Creating Scientific Communities in the Elementary Classroom

Creating Scientific Communities in the Elementary Classroom

Maureen Reddy

Patty Jacobs

Caryn McCrohon

Leslie Rupert Herrenkohl

HEINEMANN
Portsmouth, NH

Heinemann
A division of Reed Elsevier Inc.
361 Hanover Street
Portsmouth, NH 03801–3912

Offices and agents throughout the world

© 1998 by Maureen Reddy, Patty Jacobs, Caryn McCrohon, and Leslie Rupert Herrenkohl

Library of Congress Cataloging-in-Publication Data
Creating scientific communities in the elementary classroom / Maureen
    Reddy . . . [et al.].
        p. cm.
    Includes bibliographical references.
    ISBN 0-325-00008-5
    1. Science—Study and teaching (Elementary)—United States—Case
studies. 2. Group work in education—United States—Case studies.
3. College-school cooperation—United States—Case studies.
I. Reddy, Maureen, 1950–
LB1585.3.C74   1998
372.3′5′044—dc21   97-49090
                                                                 CIP

Editor: Victoria Merecki
Production: Vicki Kasabian
Cover design: Mary Cronin
Manufacturing: Louise Richardson

Printed in the United States of America on acid-free paper
02 01 00 99 98 RRD 1 2 3 4 5

Contents

Acknowledgments

This book is dedicated to Jacob Hiatt, whose remarkable generosity made the Hiatt Center for Urban Education at Clark University a reality. Like many Clark researchers and Worcester teachers, we have greatly profited from his gift.

We have also been helped by a number of other people whom we would like to thank. Five years ago Joan Merrill, with characteristic foresight, recognized the potential of our collaboration. As principal of the Goddard School of Science and Technology, she often speaks about "inviting children into learning." Her belief that a school can be a community of inquiry, for adults and children alike, has also invited us into learning.

Sarah Michaels, director of the Hiatt Center, had a key role in getting us together. Her continuing trust and warm support have given us many exciting opportunities and more faith in ourselves.

Others at Clark have also provided intellectual guidance: Jim Gee has helped us to think about Discourse (with an upper case D); Jim Wertsch, formerly at Clark but now at Washington University in St. Louis, has been pivotal in our thinking about Vygotsky; Tom Del Prete has invested countless hours in building our school-university partnership; Les Blatt has helped the Goddard staff to become better science learners and teachers.

Elizabeth Cohen, director of the Program for Complex Instruction at Stanford, has changed our thinking about classroom dynamics. Together with Dr. Cohen, Rachel Lotan, Joan Benton, and Patty Swanson have given their time and talent to helping Goddard teachers succeed with a challenging but rewarding approach that really works in diverse classrooms.

Worcester Public Schools supports many innovative programs. We especially want to mention Deputy Superintendent Dr. James Caradonio for his input and encouragement.

Many other people have helped to keep us going during the long process of creating this book. Marion Guerra, the science facilitator at Goddard, is always ready to answer a question, but more important, to offer kind words, wise advice, and generally lessen anxiety. Fellow teacher-researchers at the Goddard School have created a supportive atmosphere for our work. Susan Kaneb, Rebecca Abrahamson, and Dina Gabianelli proofread parts of the manuscript. Dina loaned her new laptop, and Dan Reddy provided computer assistance throughout.

Leslie would like to acknowledge the James S. McDonnell Foundation for postdoctoral funding, which supported her during a portion of the time that she worked on the book. She would also like to thank Annemarie Sullivan Palincsar, her postdoctoral sponsor at the University of Michigan, and Shirley Magnusson, a science educator at the University of Southern Maine, for their input throughout the writing process. In addition, Leslie is grateful to everyone at the University of Washington for their extraordinary patience and support in helping facilitate communication between the coasts. Specifically, the help of Jennifer Davis, Kent Jewell, and Jerry Purcell has been greatly appreciated.

Finally, our greatest "thank you" goes to the children of the Goddard School.

Introduction
Collaborative Learning Among Teachers and Researchers

> We can be known only in the unfolding of our unique stories within the contexts of everyday events.
>
> —Vivian Gussin Paley, *The Boy Who Would Be a Helicopter*

In this book stories of science learning will be prominent. We hope that these stories will introduce you to the children that we teach and learn from, and to us as people, as teachers, and as researchers.

As you will see throughout the book, each of us tells stories from our own perspective and in our own voice. Therefore, we have decided that the best way to tell *our* story is for each of us to provide her own viewpoint on how we got together. We all take the same starting point: a two-week-long staff development institute sponsored by the Jacob Hiatt Center for Urban Education at Clark University for the teachers at the Goddard School of Science and Technology. The focus of the institute was Complex Instruction, a cooperative learning approach that will be explained in Chapter 1. It took place in July 1992, one month before the opening of Goddard. Some of the staff members were transferring from another neighborhood school and obviously knew each other; many were meeting for the first time. All had agreed to learn and then teach the new science program, but nobody fully understood what they were getting into.

Caryn's Story

In July 1992, about a month before the Goddard School was to open, the new staff attended a two-week seminar on Complex Instruction. We were a big staff and I did not know many people, but to my relief I did know a few, including Leslie and Maureen (they were there as researchers, although I did not yet know them in this capacity).

I had met Maureen the previous February while teaching first grade. She was a consultant hired to facilitate writing in grades one though six. To this day I still use many of the strategies and techniques Maureen modeled and taught me.

Leslie was a student at Clark University working on her Ph.D. when I met her, around the same time I'd met Maureen. She was spending time in the sixth-grade classroom in preparation for choosing her dissertation topic.

On the first day of the institute, Patty sought out the teachers who were going to be her second-grade teammates. There were four of us, all strangers, and Patty was instrumental in breaking the ice. Although the second-grade team had much to talk about, I felt my experience was very limited compared to that of the others so I took a passive role during these conversations. I certainly did not want to say anything wrong in front of these veteran teachers, so I just agreed and nodded a lot. I seemed to do this frequently during the whole institute.

One reason for my hesitation was I felt that I was not very competent in the area of science. It was never my strong point in all my years of schooling. I kept quiet during the institute because I didn't want anyone to think I wouldn't be able to successfully teach science. I figured I could study up on the required grade-two curriculum during the rest of the summer. No one would have to find out about my science phobia.

Imagine how I felt when Leslie and Maureen said they wanted to come into my classroom during science to research the effectiveness of the new science program! I smiled and said yes; luckily they didn't see me kicking myself as I said it.

Maureen's Story

My role at the institute was somewhat undefined. I was not a presenter, but I had some responsibility for how things proceeded because I had recently gone to Stanford for a faculty seminar on Complex Instruction. Since I was not "on" much of the time, I could socialize freely, and somehow Patty and I talked a lot during the two weeks. It may have been that Patty didn't know the other teachers and so had more time to talk to me. Looking back, though, I know it was more than that. Some of the teachers in the workshop voiced concerns about their roles in the hands-on, meaning making teaching that was being advocated, but not Patty. Both of us drew parallels between the Complex Instruction program and whole language, since both of us had experience in child-centered reading and writing curricula. I knew, even from these preliminary conversations, that her classroom would be interesting.

I had been hired by the Hiatt Center for Urban Education at Clark to research the new science program. I thought that if Patty was comfortable with the new program she might not mind having me watch as she began using Complex Instruction. Still, I can't believe what I did. It's something that we now laugh about, something that I think is out of character for me.

I showed up on the very first day of school, a brand-new school where *everything* was new: the kids, the teachers, the routines, the bus routes, the lunch lines—everything. There I was, on the very first day of school, with a letter for Patty, a formal letter, asking if I could do research in her classroom. I had expected to leave it in her mailbox (she probably didn't even know where her mailbox was at that point) and get a phone call in a day or two. Instead I ran into her outside at recess, handed her the letter, and received her warm welcome on the spot.

When I began this collaborative project, I was a novice researcher. For four years, I had been a diligent doctoral student and in my qualitative research course I learned about "negotiating entry." I was ready to begin. At the time, I considered myself fortunate but also adept at negotiating entry. As I look back now, I appreciate how lucky I was that Patty didn't consider me way too pushy or insensitive toward the reality of schools.

I had considered approaching Caryn that first day too, but she was just beginning her first year of full-time teaching and I felt that the last thing she needed was me watching her. The problem, though, was that I wanted to work with two teachers, partly, I admit, to hedge my bets in case something happened with one of them. Only a week had passed, but the more I thought about it, the more I, as a novice, felt that the school year was slipping right by. I had seen Caryn several times in the hall and she had been very friendly. I decided to give it a try, so I asked her—without a formal letter. I went and told her that I wanted to watch, and she said it would be fine. And it has been much more than fine.

During the institute that summer I had also met and worked with Leslie. Her job was to document; mine was somewhere between participating and coteaching. There was an intensity to the institute that created a bond among all of us who worked there, but Leslie and I established a different type of rapport from the beginning. I was struck by the way that our different backgrounds often got us to a shared insight by alternate routes.

When the school year began, Leslie and I had a common mission: to answer that quintessential ethnographic question, "What's going on here?" as it pertained to the new school and the science program. Looking back, I'm sure that it's no accident that we both decided that the second grade was most interesting and that Caryn and Patty would be best to work with. Strangely, we decided this independently and at first thought that one or the other would have to find another site. Fortunately, our boss and mentor, Sarah Michaels, liked the idea of a four-way collaboration, and that's how it all began.

Leslie's Story

My role at the institute was very clear. I was employed to document it using video- and audiotapes and to collect other relevant information such as written materials that were distributed or any notes from one of the leadership team members. I had an opportunity to see all parts of the institute, including formal presentations, whole group discussions, participant collaboration to prepare for the teaching of a science unit, and informal conversations that occurred during lunches and breaks. My most salient role though was that of camera person. Teachers participating in the workshop would often tease me saying that they wouldn't know what I looked like without a camera in front of my eye. I was concerned people would dislike being videotaped, especially during the time when they actually had to teach a lesson with real kids. The videotapes of the teaching sessions gave someone from the leadership team a chance to provide feedback to the teachers, complete with examples from their actual lesson. It was a great idea in theory but obviously made some teachers nervous when they found a camera shadowing them for much of the time they were teaching. When teachers were discussing their discomfort about the videotaping, one of the them noted that it was "just Leslie" behind the camera, so they didn't have anything to be concerned about. Being "just Leslie" worked in my favor as I was able to get acquainted with many of the teachers and interview them knowing that they were not concerned about being "watched" by me. It was in this context that I first met Patty, Maureen, and Caryn.

Since part of my task was to collect participant feedback and impressions, I set out to interview people who I thought might have some reflections, comments, or critique to offer. I was also interested in finding out more about the teachers' expectations for the coming school year, when they would implement the program in their classes. Patty seemed like a perfect candidate for an interview, and I was able to do this during the first week.

For Patty the upcoming year was to be full of changes. She had not been a teacher in this public school district before, so this, in addition to the science focus, would constitute a change for her. Patty was not a novice teacher though, and expressed excitement about all the new challenges that she would face as she taught second-grade science in the diverse context of an urban elementary school. She indicated that she was looking forward to using her whole language philosophy to guide her teaching in many areas, including science. It was this experience that convinced me that she would be a wonderful person to follow during the upcoming school year.

I had met Caryn a few months before the institute, when I was a classroom volunteer in the school where she was working as a long-term substitute. When we met again at the institute, and I saw that she was going to participate, I knew I had another person on my interview list. I interviewed Caryn at lunch with some other teachers and I must admit that in addition to gathering information about the workshop, I hoped that we would continue to develop our friendship.

Maureen was a very capable researcher and a great person to work with. She was always handing me notes or copies of materials that were distributed to the teachers. She was incredibly organized and thoughtful. She was also very insightful and interested in some of the same issues and theorists that I was. But, as the beginning of the school year approached, I knew that there were only two of us but there were teachers at every grade from second through sixth, each doing multiple science units in a school with more than seven hundred students!

I felt overwhelmed with the task of documenting the implementation of the science program. I had assumed that Maureen and I would coordinate our work at the school since we were trying to accomplish the same thing, but that we would both focus our efforts in different classrooms in order to gather as much data as possible. When we discovered that we both wanted to work in the same classrooms, we were stumped about how to proceed. We both thought that in addition to Patty's and

Caryn's seemingly open attitudes toward our being in their classrooms, it would be useful to document the implementation of the science program in the second grade because it was the first year in which it was being introduced.

Thankfully Sarah allowed us to focus our efforts in the same place to describe and understand the development of second-grade scientists (and science teachers, as Patty and Caryn like to remind us). Unlike Maureen, I had never taken a course on qualitative methods and did not know the first thing about "negotiating entry" or even what to pay attention to in the organized chaos of elementary classrooms. I had much to learn about conducting ethnographic research in such settings. I learned a lot from Maureen that first year. Perhaps Sarah knew this, and this was part of the reason she supported our collaboration.

Patty's Story

As I entered Room 101 of Jonas Clark Hall at Clark University on the first day of the Complex Instruction Institute, I felt my career was about to change in ways I could not imagine and I could not wait to begin. I had spent most of my teaching years in small private schools teaching first, second, and third grades. Twenty years earlier, I had set out as a graduate student to work with children in an urban public school system. Goddard offered me a similar challenge with an equally diverse population.

I was also interested in Goddard because it would offer a literature-based reading and process writing program to its students. I had spent several years developing my skills in whole language. I was an avid reader in the field of whole language and was trying to hone my skills as a teacher of reading and writing.

I didn't worry about teaching science because I described Goddard as a school that focused on whole language. I originally believed that I would be expected to teach science somewhere during the school day on some irregular basis. I am not sure when I realized how much science I would be teaching. I imagined the science institute I was about to begin was about cooperative learning.

When I entered the room where we were gathering to begin two weeks of training in science I suddenly froze. I was faced with at least thirty new faces. Everyone seemed to be reacquainting themselves after a short break from the previous school year. The only person I knew was the principal. I took my seat and observed the room wondering how I would find my niche.

Finding a niche was important to me. I was seeking something I could not find in my previous position. At the time I could not describe what it was, but now I realize that I wanted to collaborate with other teachers.

My first conversations were with Leslie and Maureen, who were working as researchers recording the institute. Both Leslie and Maureen willingly shared ideas and thoughts they had about Complex Instruction.

When the school year began, Caryn and I both felt that Maureen and Leslie should visit unannounced during science time. With all the dynamics in our schedule it seemed overwhelming to me to have a fixed observation time. I think because I did not prepare for their visits it allowed me to feel more relaxed when they came.

As October ended during my first year at Goddard, Nancy Ellis, a member of the summer institute leadership team, came to visit. Maureen and Leslie were in my classroom that day. Nancy enjoyed her science time with us, but went on to make several suggestions for changes. I responded by completely "melting down" as Maureen and Leslie tried to encourage me not to give up.

One of Nancy's concerns was that many children were not wearing badges to designate their assigned roles. The paper ones that I made at the beginning of the school year had already worn out. Role badges help things to run smoothly, and Nancy was again trying to explain why. Leslie was particularly concerned about my distress and quickly went out to buy oak tag. She and Maureen made me a new set of name tags. I was thankful for their support but even more thankful because I had found a new niche and they were helping me feel at home in this large new school.

The Goddard School of Science and Technology

Our collaboration has been influenced by the many people we have met and worked with and the experiences we have had over our years as students, teachers, and researchers. We come from different backgrounds and experiences: Patty and Caryn both participated in teacher preparation programs at the bachelor's and master's levels. Leslie has been trained as a developmental psychologist throughout her B.A., M.A., and Ph.D. years. Maureen was a student of English literature and classics as an undergraduate, received a masters in education in Language Arts, and then earned an Ed.D. in language and literacy. In spite of these differences, we all share a common focus and vision regarding teaching and learning in school settings, one that is widely shared among many of our colleagues in the Clark University—Worcester Public Schools Collaborative, and especially at the Goddard School, which is our teaching and research site.

Situated in the south quadrant of Worcester, the city's poorest and most troubled neighborhood, Goddard is the latest incarnation of a century old building that was first a high school, later a middle school, and

now houses the approximately eight hundred children who attend the
largest public elementary school in New England's second largest city. The
science program, a major feature of Goddard's attraction as a magnet
school, is described in a pamphlet that outlines the various school programs for parents who are choosing a school: "The teaching of science
. . . is characterized by open-ended inquiry, a focus on the development
of higher order thinking skills, and small group problem solving tasks that
require multiple intellectual abilities." This description highlights a type
of cooperative learning called Complex Instruction, which will be explained in the next chapter.

As a "neighborhood magnet school," Goddard welcomes children
who live in the neighborhood and also attracts students from throughout
the city as part of a voluntary deisolation plan. A very rich racial, ethnic,
and socioeconomic mix of students is the result. In thirty-five classrooms
from preschool through grade six, Goddard has a population that is about
half children of color. About one quarter are in a Spanish bilingual
program. Approximately ninety percent qualify for free or reduced lunch.

Goddard is also a close neighbor of Clark University and is now
a Professional Development School in the Clark University—Worcester
Public Schools Collaborative. Goddard's principal, Dr. Joan Merrill, was a
primary architect of this school university partnership along with Dr.
Sarah Michaels, director of the Jacob Hiatt Center for Urban Education,
and more recently, Dr. Thomas Del Prete, chair of the Education Depart-
ment at Clark.

1 *The Importance of Talking and Writing in Science*

One brain isn't better than all the brains together.

— J. P., a second grader

I take the perspective that learning is a process of transformation of participation.

— Barbara Rogoff

The two quotes above are juxtaposed for a reason. Although one was spoken by a second grader and the other was written by a world famous developmental psychologist, they both eloquently describe the learning situations that we try to create for children, as well as the context of our work together as adults.

This book is a collaboration across communities and across discourses as two teachers and two academic researchers think and write together. It is based on teacher research, participant research, and a five-yearlong teacher/researcher partnership. While promoting group work among children, we have proven J. P.'s words true time and time again, as our collaboration has both charged and changed our thinking. Similarly, Barbara Rogoff's words apply to the children whom we teach and study, since we attempt to help them see themselves as full participants in science. Her words apply equally to us as we have taken on multiple new collaborative roles as observers, learners, teachers, researchers, and writers.

We are not scientists, or trained science educators, so we also have depended on each other to learn more science, including concepts, procedures, and attitudes. Over the years we've looked things up, consulted scientists and other teachers, and experimented with the materials the children use. We feel that this book can speak to the many teachers and academic researchers who, like us, are interested in science teaching and learning, but often do not have strong science backgrounds themselves. This book will concentrate on language and literacy in science through

1

stories, transcripts, and children's writing. Although we use many examples of children talking and writing about their hands-on activities, our emphasis is not on the activities themselves.

As elementary school teachers, Patty and Caryn are particularly interested in literacy; Leslie and Maureen's research pays special attention to language. It is natural, therefore, that we have documented what teachers and children say and write in science classes in an effort to understand the development of early scientific literacy.

In spite of our differences, we all share a common focus and vision regarding teaching and learning in school settings. Our common philosophy is perhaps best exemplified through the work of the Russian psychologist Vygotsky, who wrote, "children solve practical tasks with the help of their speech as well as their eyes and hands" (Vygotsky 1978, 26).

Theoretical Framework

Vygtosky worked during the early part of this century to understand human development and learning. His writings first appeared in English in 1962, and since that time they have come to play an important role in much of the current thinking about education (Tharp and Gallimore 1988; Wertsch 1985; Moll 1990). Vygotsky was specifically interested in educational contexts and spent much of his life theorizing about and researching children's learning within this setting. One important point that sets Vygotsky apart from Piaget and other developmental theorists influential in education is his claim that thinking and speaking are intimately related. However, Vygotsky did not believe that speaking was the verbal expression of thought. He viewed thinking and speaking as distinct lines of development up to a certain point where "speech becomes intellectual and thinking verbal" (Vygotsky 1987, 117). In his view this is the ultimate accomplishment of human beings. From his perspective many psychologists had demonstrated that animals did in fact have rudimentary thought processes that allowed them to solve problems. What they did not have is a social form of communication that would transform and elevate their thinking to a new level. Vygotsky strongly believed that the basis of human thinking resides in this kind of social life. This tenet is the cornerstone of his theory and is manifested in many ways throughout his research. He writes, "human learning presupposes a specific social nature and a process by which children grow into the intellectual life of those around them" (1978, 88). In other words, he believed something that is radically different from Western cultural perspectives, which suggest that the starting point for any investigation of development should be the individual. Vygotsky, on the other hand, argues that any inquiry into human learning and development must start with social processes first.

An essential feature of these social process, in his view, was speech, as he argues, "the development of the child's thinking depends on his mastery of the social means of thinking, that is, on his mastery of speech" (Vygotsky 1987, 120). Thus, Vygotsky makes claims about human learning taking place first in the social sphere and only later manifesting itself on the individual level.

It might now be a bit clearer why Vygotsky was so interested in speech. Speech is essential to human social interaction. It is one important way that we communicate with others around us. For Vygotsky it was perhaps the most important "cultural tool" that humans have developed to facilitate such interaction. We accept Vygotsky's social approach to thinking and believe that students need ample opportunities to talk and discuss their budding ideas in school settings. To many teachers this may seem self-evident, but we believe as educators that we have yet to fully grapple with the challenges that arise when we try to put this pedagogical philosophy to work in real classrooms, especially in content areas outside of the language arts.

Take science for example. There have been many programs that have advocated hands-on approaches. These have been truly influential in thinking about teaching science, particularly when working with young children. They have prompted a movement toward helping students construct their own understanding of phenomena, rather than receiving knowledge through textbooks. In spite of this benefit we have also noticed that these programs encourage students to experiment with materials without insuring that they have opportunities to talk about these experiences. Many of these programs implicitly assume that children are building knowledge through their interactions with the materials and other children alone. We believe that giving students a collection of interesting materials to manipulate does not necessarily translate into a deep level of understanding about how to use the materials and what to pay attention to when putting them to use. Furthermore, such opportunities do not guarantee that students are engaged in building conceptual understanding in science. Our focus therefore will not be on activities in science, although we believe that well designed activities are absolutely essential. Rather, we will emphasize the role of talk and teacher support in providing students with opportunities to begin to build understanding together in the classroom community.

Within school settings, as in many others, speech is an important way that people communicate their ideas to one another. Although speech sometimes functions to convey a message from one person to another, it is rarely as straightforward as the metaphor of a telephone with a caller and a receiver. Communication is in large part a process of constructing meaning together, not being the sender or receiver of a static message.

Barnes and Todd (1995) aptly describe this process as thus: "Meaning is not something owned by one participant in a discussion but something that, developing and changing as it does in the course of a series of contributions by different participants, is constructed and reconstructed by all of them" (141). This process of meaning construction is something that will be demonstrated over and over throughout this book, as we offer examples of Caryn and Patty talking and writing with their students. It is through such processes that they have an opportunity to help students understand scientific ways of using materials, and also support children to articulate what they find interesting about such experimentation. In their classrooms this practice of constructing and reconstructing meaning also provides the basis for shared classroom values as well as shared conceptual understandings.

Establishing shared meaning at the classroom level is not only crucial for constructing understanding as a group, it is an essential step in allowing students to build and solidify meaning for themselves. In other words, we argue that group discussion and meaning making leads ultimately to individual learning and competence. This is a crucial part of Vygotsky's theory. Speech functions not only as a communicative device but also as a tool for individuals to use when regulating their own thinking. Thus, speech forms a link between social life and individual intellectual functioning. Vygotsky calls this kind of speech "inner speech" or "social speech turned inward" (1978, 27). If you have ever needed a reason to legitimize talking to yourself, Vygotsky's theory provides plenty of support.

If speech functions both to communicate and to regulate one's own thinking, how do these functions relate to one another in classroom life? How does social communication become transformed into individual student thinking? How can teachers facilitate this process? Courtney Cazden (1988) addresses these questions by suggesting that teachers can use dialogue with students as a "scaffold" to support them as they build on their current level of competence and understanding. She uses the analogy of a child learning how to walk. At first an adult may offer two hands to aid the child as she moves her feet, later only one hand is needed and offered, then just a finger, and finally no support is necessary for the child to walk on her own. Gradually reducing the level of assistance provides an opportunity for the child to develop the complex skill of walking. It is much the same with students who are learning within classrooms. At first teachers offer help and guidance through questioning, probing, and modeling, and as the students become more capable of completing tasks on their own, fewer and fewer prompts are needed. This approach is not recitation-based (Mehan 1979) where language serves as a device to transmit knowledge to students, rather it is more like an "apprenticeship" (Rogoff 1990) with language functioning to guide students as they build their own knowledge that eventually leads them to accomplish tasks on their own.

Vygtosky (1978) talks about this process as working within a student's "Zone of Proximal Development" (86). He argues that it is important to recognize not only what students can achieve on their own, but also what they are capable of completing with the help of a teacher or more competent peer. This kind of approach anticipates what children are on the verge of mastering, rather than focusing on what they can already do. The Zone of Proximal Development is a useful concept because often it is not very helpful for teachers to know what students can already accomplish on their own. What they need to know in planning future instruction is what is within children's reach but not yet mastered. In order to anticipate students' learning, teachers must seek opportunities to listen to what the students are saying and determine what they are struggling with and what kind of assistance might help them. It is very difficult to plan for classroom activities that involve such extensive amounts of listening to student speech, reading student writing, and supporting student thinking. It is messy, unpredictable, and requires that teachers react and respond on-line to the ideas, issues, and concerns raised by students. Rather than the Initiation-Response-Evaluation (IRE) pattern that is frequently observed in classrooms, this kind of talk focuses on genuine questions and extended discussions among teachers and students. Students frequently feel comfortable saying "I don't know" and teachers must find ways to help them continue to build their knowledge so that they come to know. Furthermore, it requires an understanding of how children construct knowledge in addition to an understanding of important aspects of the disciplinary content at the center of instruction. This is a tall order for teachers. It requires a tremendous amount of energy and effort. But, at the same time, we hope to demonstrate that it also provides an exciting and rewarding environment for teachers and students (and researchers) alike.

This pedagogical philosophy based on Vygotskian theory permeates our work together and the general themes discussed in this section provide the background for all that we write about throughout this book.

Complex Instruction

Frequently it can be difficult for teachers to reconcile a theoretical stance with the daily realities of classroom life. This may be why there is often a rift between theory and practice. We have said that we consider social interaction and many forms of student talk to be essential for children's learning. But how can teachers enact this theory and orchestrate classroom activities in such a way that children are productively engaged with materials, with each other in small and large groups, and with their teacher? Complex Instruction has provided Patty and Caryn with a structure that allows them to do this.

When visitors walk into Patty's and Caryn's classrooms they will see a collection of brightly colored signs the teachers have made that signal that they are using Complex Instruction. This program, designed by Dr. Elizabeth Cohen, a Stanford University sociologist, has been adopted schoolwide at Goddard. Complex Instruction is an approach that allows teachers to teach at a high level in very heterogeneous classrooms, managing active learning across a variety of subjects. At Goddard, a Complex Instruction science program is in place for grades two through six.

Complex Instruction has been a fruitful site for us to research and think about science teaching and learning. Caryn and Patty have found that the structure of this program has given them a way to organize their classrooms and to teach large, diverse classes of children doing open-ended activities. Complex Instruction includes hands-on exploration with attention to social dynamics and special emphasis on equity. However, it is equally important to appreciate that the practices that we describe and the insights that we have gained are much more widely applicable than any program. We are not promoting a particular method since there are many good science programs and curricula available, but rather we advocate time and support for children's science talk and writing against a backdrop of rich activities.

Complex Instruction is a type of cooperative learning that has some special features as well as many similarities to other types of cooperative learning. For instance, it involves roles for the children to play. One is facilitator, whose job is to see to it that everyone understands the activity and that everyone participates. The child who performs this role does not have to be a good reader, but he or she must ensure that the directions are read to everyone's satisfaction. This is a complicated role since some beginning second graders see the facilitator as "the boss" with more rights than responsibilities.

Another key role is that of reporter. This is the person who, at the end of the activity, delivers a report from the group, telling the whole class what they did. Both Patty and Caryn structure this role in such a way that the reporter gets input and help from group members. Nevertheless, it is the reporter who must tell what happened in the group. As we will explain and illustrate in later chapters, this is also a complicated role for seven-year-olds because they are not speaking for themselves as individuals, rather they are representing their groups.

A third role, one that is enjoyed greatly by the second graders, is that of materials manager. The materials manager goes to get the equipment or supplies, checks to be sure that the group has what it needs, and doles them out equitably. Many of our colleagues tell us that older kids think of this as a low-status occupation, but in second grade, if you control the materials, you've got power.

Another important role is that of cleanup manager. The class often discusses the fact that everybody helps this person, whose task it is to oversee the cleanup after the activity is over. Having a role for this task means it usually gets done in a timely fashion so there is enough time left at the end of the period for a group discussion.

In Complex Instruction the roles are procedural, enabling children to accomplish their group tasks. The roles do not divide the labor of the task itself, nor do they specify special skills such as "artist" or "reader." Roles are assigned randomly and they rotate so that every child has a chance to play each role several times throughout the year. Even shy children will get up to report and reticent students will facilitate the groups.

Successful role playing does not happen easily or automatically. Caryn, Patty, and their students frequently talk about and work with the roles. This time is well spent because the roles help the teacher to maintain well functioning groups that can do most of the more mundane management for themselves, thus freeing Patty and Caryn for the more demanding and interesting tasks of carefully observing or intervening in the groups with provocative questions or suggestions.

Another aspect of the Complex Instruction design which frees the teacher from minute to minute management is the emphasis on cooperative norms. They are simply rules for behavior that make groups function smoothly. Such norms are certainly not unique to Complex Instruction, and in fact are in place, whether implicitly or explicitly, in all well managed classrooms. Sometimes, though, norms that operate in other classrooms, or even in other parts of our school day, are in conflict with the expectations for group work, for instance, students are often asked not to talk, or to give advice to others. During science, we especially want children to talk and listen to one another, to share their work and ideas, and to pay attention to others' needs. Some of the norms that we emphasize speak to group work in a focused way, for instance: "You have the right to ask anyone in your group for help." Of course, as you might expect, just as we can't take it for granted that children will play their roles, we also cannot assume that hanging signs on the walls will change their behavior, so Goddard teachers work hard at embedding these norms in classroom life. In the chapters that follow you will read many examples of Caryn and Patty discussing these norms with children. We have come to see also that these norms are not just about classroom management, though they are crucial for a smoothly functioning classroom. They also have to do with acquiring "habits of mind" that are compatible with scientific literacy.

A typical Complex Instruction lesson is structured much like writers' workshop. Instead of a minilesson at the beginning, there is an orientation of about ten minutes. Topics run the gamut from how to hold a measuring tape to a review of the roles or the introduction of some necessary vocabulary. At the beginning of a unit, orientation often takes the form of an open-ended science talk (Gallas 1995) when children will simply discuss whatever they know or wonder about a topic. For instance, before they began a unit on measurement, Patty's children had a talk during which they could say whatever came to mind when they thought of measurement. Here are some of their comments that were recorded on chart paper:

> You can measure yourself. You can mark off where your head leaves off and then you look at the wall to see how tall you are.

> You can measure Mrs. Jacobs. You could stand on the end of a tape measure and pull it up to the top of her head.

> You can measure a little tree. Take a big measure and measure it.

> You can measure a big tree but you would need a friend to do it.

> You could climb the tree with a tape measure in your pocket and drop the heavy end.

> You don't always need a ruler.

> You can measure your wrist. You take a tape measure and go around to see how big it is.

> You can measure with your sight.

> Estimate is like guessing.

> You could measure your body with a rope and then you could use that rope to measure something else.

> A lot of people like to measure cuz it's fun.

As a unit progresses, Patty and Caryn will seize teaching opportunities, raising issues or topics in orientation that have emerged from the previous day's groupwork or wrap-up. After the orientation, the children disperse into heterogeneous groups of four or five students for an activity time that usually lasts about one half hour.

Finally, children all clean up and come together to share what they've done in wrap-up. This time is structured, with Caryn and Patty moderating the discussion, but the children take the lead in introducing topics. In other words, they know that the reporters all come up and stand next to the teacher, and that they must tell "what happened" in the group, but from all the things that did happen, they can select whatever they found interesting. The range of topics at wrap-up is very wide. Much of what we share in this book will be based upon the interaction in wrap-up because we feel that it is so important.

For the activities, Patty and Caryn use curriculum that is designed to work with the Complex Instruction system. Its principal features are that the activities are open-ended, require multiple abilities, are organized around a big idea or theme, and not sequentially structured. The lack of sequence is important because from the first day, each group does a different activity. Then the groups rotate so that by the end of a unit each group will have done each task. These rotations through a series of activities that are thematically connected result in conceptual redundancy, meaning that children have several opportunities to understand the concepts. Each task is a slightly different vantage point on the same "big idea," allowing children to catch on at their own rate of learning.

Once groups have settled into their work, Caryn and Patty can circulate among them, taking notice of what's going well or poorly and nudging children toward developing their theories about the science content. They both take notes about what they observe, to mention during wrap-up—sometimes about how well children are cooperating or playing their roles, sometimes about the science content. Good anecdotal notes enable them to provide very specific feedback to children about group functioning or about individual contributions. Such record keeping also provides documentation of what took place for future reference or for assessment.

One feature of Complex Instruction that is distinct from other types of cooperative learning is attention to status. According to Elizabeth Cohen:

> Small task groups tend to develop hierarchies where some members are more active and influential than others. This is a *status ordering* [emphasis in original]—an agreed-upon social ranking where everyone feels it is better to have a high rank within the status order than a low rank. (1994, 27)

In other words, when given rich hands-on tasks, some children will dominate while others will be left out. According to Cohen, a sociologist, this happens because they have lower status and are perceived to be less able to contribute (1984). Such perceptions are often not accurate, but they are pervasive. For many children at the second-grade level, reading ability is the most powerful status characteristic, with math aptitude not far behind. If you can't read, other kids think that you're not smart, even though you may have many other relevant abilities. The fact that high status children dominate is a problem for teachers because those who are excluded will learn less and those who take over will have an unfair advantage (Cohen, Lotan, and Catanzarite 1990).

Knowledge of Complex Instruction has sensitized us to these social forces within groups. Some children who are shut out may become disruptive; others may retreat. Armed with this new insight about the impact of status, Patty and Caryn do not necessarily blame them for the problem, but rather seek a group solution. Instead of just thinking that a child is unmotivated or shy, they observe the interaction very carefully. They try to look more deeply into the group dynamic to see if students who are not actively participating are being prevented from doing so. This is a new vantage point for educators because we have historically thought more in terms of psychology and the characteristics of individuals, like self-concept or fear of failure. Complex Instruction has taught Caryn and Patty a strategy for adjusting the status order in the classroom, a technique called "assigning competence." Assigning competence is based on close observation of the child who is having a problem, as well as the other children in the group. It is based on a theory of multiple abilities, or as Cohen says, "There are many ways to be smart."

During orientations, the teachers talk about the different abilities that will be necessary to successfully complete the tasks. While observing groups, the teachers try to appreciate what the child is doing that displays an ability, whether it is fine motor control in tying a knot, or precision in drawing. Then, they point out to the rest of the group (or the whole class) what that child did that was helpful to their peers and why. They also relate it to an ability which the children might not have recognized on their own. The goal is for others to see the low-status child as a potentially valuable group member who has an important contribution to make. When Patty and Caryn do this, the children pay attention for two reasons: first, they value their teacher's opinion, and second, Caryn and Patty are always truthful and specific about the child's contribution. It can be very frustrating if there is a child that you really want to help but they just don't do anything that can be talked about. However, it is absolutely imperative that the feedback is authentic if this technique is to work. We will offer many different examples of children who have become much more valued in their groups and thus active in our classrooms because Patty and Caryn have been able to "assign competence" to them.

Description of Data and Transcription

Many of the examples we have used will be presented as transcripts of classroom talk. Most are from wrap-up, with a few from orientations and groupwork. To make these transcripts more readable, we have used standard punctuation and eliminated most technical marks with the exception of pauses: three dots [. . .] indicate a short pause and the words (long pause) indicate just that. We have used standard spelling for most speech except where children's natural pronunciation was easy to convey, for instance such words as "cuz" for because and "gonna" for going to. Patty and Caryn would like readers to take note of the fact that transcripts represent oral language with all of its false starts, misspoken words, and phrases. Any readers who have seen transcripts of their own talk will realize that when you first read what you said, you often can't believe how inarticulate you are. However, natural classroom dialogue is messy and it is constructed on-line. In the talk that we have captured, teachers are not delivering well wrought speeches; they are engaging in conversations. We believe that the hesitations and false starts, the ums and ahs that we have left in, are an important part of these examples because they show teachers and children thinking on their feet.

In the transcripts, different turns are labeled with the name of the speaker unless they are unable to be identified, in which case we simply call him or her "child." As a way to clearly differentiate transcripts from dialogue journal entries, we have marked turns in journals by putting the teacher's writing in italics and the child's writing in regular type. For ease of reading, we have standardized spelling and punctuation in journal entries.

As you read, you may notice that the examples are not evenly distributed between Patty's and Caryn's classrooms. There are more of Caryn's examples. This is the case for two reasons. First, Patty was Hiatt Fellow at Clark for a full school year, during which she was out of the classroom, attending classes at Clark and working on special projects at Goddard. During this year, Maureen and Leslie continued to visit Caryn's classroom and collect data. Also, Caryn came up with the idea of dialogue journals in science, and began using them well before Patty did, so we have more examples of written conversations from her class. The examples that you will read, however, are representative of the practices and atmosphere of both classrooms.

2 Acquiring Scientific Habits of Mind in a Learning Community

Sam kept a dairy—a daybook about his life. It was just a cheap notebook that was always by his bed. Every night, before he turned in, he would write in the book. He wrote about things he had done, things he had seen, and thoughts he had had. Sometimes he drew a picture. He always ended by asking himself a question so he would have something to think about while falling asleep.

—E. B. White, *The Trumpet of the Swan*

In E. B. White's novel *The Trumpet of the Swan*, Sam ended his journal entry with a question. Although a few years older than the children whom Patty and Caryn teach, Sam is a wonderful role model for their young learners because he is curious about the world and how it works. This kind of curiosity is one of the scientific "habits of mind" that are outlined in *Benchmarks for Science Literacy* (1993) and *Science for All Americans* (1990). Both of these publications are outcomes of Project 2061, an American Association for the Advancement of Science initiative that is designed to provide a framework for learning in science, mathematics, and technology.

According to *Science for All Americans*, habits of mind "relate directly to a person's outlook on knowledge and learning and ways of thinking and acting." They list such things as understanding "the importance of verifiable data, testable hypotheses, and predictability in science" (172). We see these habits of mind operating in the classroom when, like Sam, children show a willingness to ask questions, to make connections, to understand what others are saying, and to invest time, care, effort, and determination as they try to make sense of their science activities.

In the next chapter we illustrate some of the complexities of hands-on cooperative learning in second grade. In subsequent chapters we discuss science talk and writing and children's attempts at making connections

2–1 Determination pays off

between science in school and what they observe in the world around them. All of these different aspects of our science program, however, revolve around the notion of habits of mind. This chapter is somewhat theoretical, presenting a set of beliefs that will provide a foundation for understanding what we discuss throughout the rest of the book.

Habits of Mind and Thoughtfulness

Traditionally, education has emphasized the importance of knowledge and to some degree skills. For the most part, values and attitudes have not been explicitly emphasized in schools. With regard to science, the classroom has been a place where information is transmitted as discrete facts and formulas. Or, at the other extreme, students are not given facts but rather interesting materials which are supposed to help them *discover* important scientific ideas. Neither of these two models of teaching and learning works well in our view because they do not recognize that science, as practiced by real scientists, involves a set of values. We therefore see habits of mind as a crucial concept because it forces us to recognize that teaching science involves helping students to understand and adopt the values and attitudes associated with science. An early proponent of this position was John Dewey, who argued against schooling as a place for transmitting knowledge to children. He advocated a philosophy that involves embedding knowledge in the "real world" where values are central. He believed that it was within this context that students developed understanding that was meaningful to them. In addressing the American Association for the Advancement of Science in 1909, Dewey discussed the importance of using materials and activities that help students develop scientific attitudes and promote the use of important skills. He said, "Science has been taught too much as an accumulation of ready-made material with which students are to be made familiar, not enough as a method of thinking, an attitude of mind, after the pattern of which mental habits are to be transformed" (Dewey 1910, 122). He went on to stress the importance of students learning to "search for evidence before anything passes from the realm of opinion, guess work and dogma into that of knowledge" (126). Supporting ideas with evidence is an extremely important value within the scientific community. When students actively engage in supporting their perspectives with evidence this general value associated with science has been adopted by them as a personal "habit of mind."

Habits of mind are complex because they sit at the intersection of several constructs that are hard to explicitly define—or at least have many different definitions: values and attitudes, knowledge, understanding, and skills. You are probably already aware that these concepts have a variety of meanings. Taking this confusion into account, we want to be explicit about what habits of mind means to us. From our perspective, habits of mind are synonymous with attitudes and with what some educators now call dispositions. For example, Onosko and Newmann (1994) discuss three domains that are relevant to learning in any discipline. The first is knowledge, the second is skills, and the third is dispositions of thoughtfulness. They argue that "good thinking" involves all three components, making it more than acquiring an extensive collection of facts. Their definition of knowledge includes specific subject matter content in addition to a general understanding about how information is organized and evaluated in a given subject area. For example, if we consider a child learning to read, knowledge of sound-symbol relationships and of the purposes of print are foundations. By skills Onosko and Newmann are referring to strategies that students use to apply their knowledge to solve unfamiliar problems. They are cognitive processes that put knowledge to work. For example, a child learning to read ideally will develop multiple strategies for figuring out unknown words, incorporating semantic, syntactic, graphophonemic, and pragmatic cues. In using the term dispositions they discuss particular "character traits" or attitudes that make students likely to apply their knowledge and skills in a meaningful way (29). For example, a child learning to read will truly become a reader when he chooses books of interest and reads for his own purposes.

Although Onosko and Newmann discuss knowledge, skills, and

attitudes across domains, our emphasis is on how these concepts can be applied to the teaching and learning of science. In his book *The Nature of Science,* Aicken (1991) discusses these same ideas. He claims that prospective scientists need what he calls a minimum fund of scientific knowledge but he goes on to say that "It is the skill in making use of the knowledge, not the knowledge itself, which matters" (130). He also talks about the scientific attitude: "It is the restless, probing, ever shifting search for truth which characterizes science, and not the truths that the search occasionally discovers" (125).

Onosko and Newmann clearly agree with Aicken when they suggest that "without dispositions of thoughtfulness, neither knowledge nor the skills for applying knowledge are likely to be used intelligently" (30). A foundation of knowledge and a repertoire of skills are both essential, but without the appropriate attitudes, children are not likely to even take advantage of whatever knowledge or skills that they might have.

Despite the fact that we agree with the main thrust of Onosko and Newmann's argument, we have a concern that they discuss dispositions as though they exist only within individuals. Based on Vygotskian theory, we believe that habits of mind will first develop socially as the values that are shared among people, and later will be internalized as attitudes or dispositions that exist within individuals. Likewise, Tishman, Perkins, and Jay (1995) claim that "Dispositions are acquired within and influenced by the context of a cultural environment. Everyday experience indicates that dispositions are cultivated all the time by social interaction, a key aspect of enculturation" (41).

In other words, attitudes or dispositions develop in an environment which exemplifies and promotes certain shared values, and the attitudes acquired by individuals reflect the values and norms of those communities. A teacher cannot give students habits of mind, but he or she can create an atmosphere in which they can be fostered because dispositions are patterns of thinking and behaving that are not learned through transmission but rather through practice in a supportive social environment. This is true not only for classrooms, but for any profession or discipline—like the scientific community that Aicken discusses.

If teachers are to truly understand and be able to promote habits of mind that can be integral to good thinking in science, they must understand what the shared values of a scientific community might be and how these values can be instantiated in a classroom. The question then is how do we identify such values and make them focal aspects of classroom culture and learning so that children can develop dispositions that characterize scientific habits of mind?

Science for All Americans (1990) argues that science exemplifies values that exist in society at large:

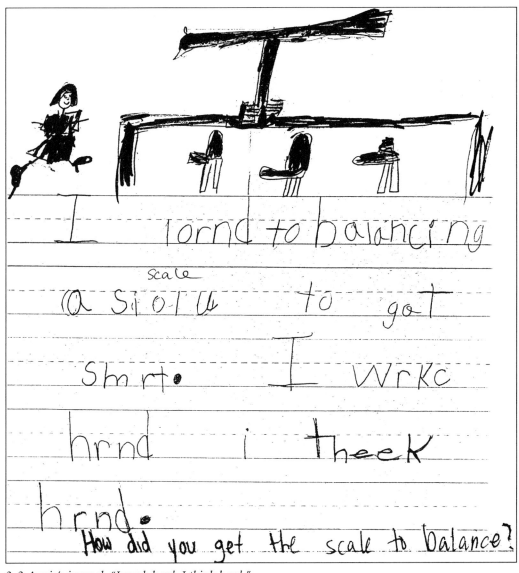

2–2 Annie's journal: "I work hard. I think hard."

Indeed, science is in many respects the systematic application of some highly regarded human values—integrity, diligence, fairness, curiosity, openness to new ideas, skepticism, and imagination. Scientists did not invent any of these values, and they are not the only people who hold them. But the broad field of science does incorporate and emphasize such values and dramatically demonstrates just how important they are for advancing human knowledge and welfare. (173)

It is true that values associated with science mirror those that are held by society more generally, yet we feel that some are more closely and specifically connected to the discipline of science. What are these attitudes or dispositions that are important in the scientific community and also might be important in a science classroom? They include a desire for claims to be well supported by evidence, a tendency to define and reflect on problems, an inquisitiveness about novel situations or unexpected outcomes, a willingness to weigh multiple perspectives on one issue, and patience and perseverance in the face of difficulty.

It is not enough to tell children about the values that scientists hold. As we emphasized in the previous chapter, we share a Vygotskian perspective that would suggest that values are transformed into attitudes when they become tools that children use to regulate their own thinking. We believe that it is necessary to have students engaged in doing, talking, and writing about science in such a way that they not only construct knowledge about scientific concepts or acquire skills in the processes of science, but also adopt attitudes that are associated with the shared values of science.

Although the creation of a community that holds certain shared social values is necessary, within such a community there are many ways that this transition to individual attitudes can be supported.

Patty's Story: Growing into a Learning Community

Are we going to do science today?

—Maria, a second grader

Maria asked this question with eager anticipation first thing in the morning, even though science time was not until the afternoon. She did not always look forward to science. In fact, she sometimes could be found under the table playing with science materials, stating firmly "I don't want to work in a group I want to work by myself!" Maria was not alone in this dilemma. Working in groups, making a plan, and being responsible for a finished group task is challenging for beginning second graders. Like all second graders, Maria is a social being at the edge of leaving

2–3 Maria collaborating

her egocentric years and entering the world of cooperating with peers. Caroline Pratt, founder of The City and Country School in New York City, refers to second grade as "a growing up year" in her book, *I Learn from Children* (1948): "Children do not grow up all of a piece; look for the child of seven, especially, to take many backward glances at the way he has come, while he bounds and leaps unevenly ahead in his growth" (87).

Lucy Calkins agrees with Caroline Pratt that second grade is a transitional year, one that Calkins calls "a land of opposites." In her book *The Art of Teaching Writing* (1986) she explains that some second graders write with what she calls "carefree confidence." However she goes on to say that "In other second grades children slowly mark their names onto their pages. If the pencil slips, causing one letter to slant against its neighbor, the youngster discards the entire page, slowly and carefully beginning yet another paper, another false start" (67).

This contradictory behavior of seven-year-olds has certainly been my experience as I have watched students hesitate when they realize their responsibility in science groups. At times they want to control the materials, to have everything done their way; at other times, they are willing to listen to and share with others. During my years as a first-grade teacher I watched six-year-olds intently engaged in parallel work and play, focused on their jobs side by side, sometimes sharing materials, but rarely talking about their tasks. I have a different set of expectations for my second graders and introduce a new set of values to them. I am asking them to participate and interact in several ways to solve problems. This kind of collaboration is new for them and at times there are children, like Maria, who would love to work or play with the materials by themselves instead of joining with other group members to solve a task. Although some students find it difficult, we persevere because we place a high value on having children talk and work together. One reason for this priority is that it is common for scientists to collaborate and come to new understandings by building upon each other's ideas. According to Deanna Kuhn, "Those seeking to understand the evolution of scientific thought have tended to focus on the lone scientist, to the exclusion of the social exchange that is the arena in which these ideas are articulated, questioned, clarified, defended, elaborated, and indeed often arise in the first place" (1993, 321). Therefore, one of the shared values that is a foundation of our science program is collaboration.

During my years teaching science, I have waited and watched the children in my room, looking for their "growing up year." The hesitation and "false starts" that they experience eventually evolve into the eager anticipation that Maria expresses in her question, "Are we going to do science today?" Maria's hesitation slowly becomes an issue of the past as she grapples with other second graders, talking, planning, and deciding how to solve the task that her small group is given. Maria eventually looks forward to working with a group in science because she has learned strategies for working with others. Maria's question indicates the development of an important attitude toward learning that comes from having participated in many previous science lessons with her classmates. It represents not only an attitude of curiosity that we want to nurture, but a shift in her original disposition toward learning in this context. Because Maria and her classmates have learned to value working together, they will persevere in problem solving activities that present a challenge to them as individuals.

This kind of transformation takes time—for children and for their teachers. Just as Maria was learning what it means to become a member of a school science community, so was I. I was learning more about the science content as well as how to facilitate productive classroom experiences for my students. Science was a new area for me. Prior to joining the faculty at Goddard, I had taught for several years, but I had not spent very much time thinking about science and in fact I was somewhat apprehensive about teaching hands-on science. I knew that science materials were no longer to be left on a corner table to be observed and used as a learning station, as they had been in some of my previous classrooms. In the beginning I was busy with all the details of understanding a new content area. Clark University Physics Professor S. Leslie Blatt (Les) and Marion Guerra, our school's science facilitator, offered a yearlong course at Goddard to help teachers strengthen skills and understanding of science, especially the science included in the units that our students will study. In this class we had an opportunity to explore the science content as learners. We constructed, poured, measured, balanced, recorded and reported results, and learned to build our ideas together. As my science background strengthened, and as I enjoyed opportunities to collaborate with other adults, I began to focus on the dynamics of groupwork.

I discovered that I was aiming for something more than what I then understood as cooperative learning. What I really wanted to see was collaboration. Cooperation does not necessarily entail collaboration. Students can share materials and help each other complete tasks without ever deeply discussing what they are doing. Collaborative problem solving requires that students demonstrate a level of interdependence in both the procedural aspect of getting the task accomplished, as well as arriving either at shared understanding or perhaps even acceptance that they have conflicting theories to account for what was observed. During the Complex Instruction Staff Development Institute we had discussed many aspects of groupwork, including interdependence among group members. However, I did not understand the role of interdependence in groups until I was in the classroom where six groups of children were trying to work together to solve scientific problems. The collaborative approach I was advocating in my class relied on children to depend on and involve all group members to plan, complete a task, and draw some conclusions together. I found that in order for the students to come to rely on one another, I had to step out of the middle and allow students to manage their own groups.

But how? This question plagued me my first year at Goddard. I was used to being the center point of everything going on in my classroom. As I look back I realize I often hovered over my students, orchestrating each move, asking questions that would focus the children on what I thought was important. Just as Maria hesitated to be in the group, I hesitated to step out. I needed to convince myself that my students could work productively by being interdependent on each other, not dependent on me. Just as Maria was growing up, I realized this was a "growing up year" for me as well. There were many elements that I needed to rethink about my teaching. How could I manage five to six groups all doing something different, or better still, how could the groups manage themselves? How could I determine when to ask questions and how to guide students through the complex process of collaborative problem solving? I discovered over time that shared values are the underpinning of our work together and the key to students developing productive attitudes toward learning. If children understand the value of working with and listening to each other, then groupwork in science will be productive.

Although it took me a long time to understand the crucial role that shared values play in the development of learning communities, this realization set a new tone in my classroom.

Shared values are closely related to a component of the Complex Instruction program which Elizabeth Cohen (1994) calls norms. As we explained in the previous chapter, norms are explicit rules for behavior that are prominently posted, frequently discussed, and then expected of students. Here is a partial list of those that I use in my classroom:

Explain by telling how and why.

Give reasons for your ideas.

Find out what others think.

Discuss and decide.

No one of us is as smart as all of us together.

You have the right to ask anyone in your group for help.

You have the duty to assist anyone who asks for help.

Help other group members without doing their work for them.

Without social norms, cooperative learning groups will not have much success. With my new insight about groupwork, I now take this a step further because I realize norms not only facilitate positive behavior, but, as shared values, can translate into student attitudes. One norm I emphasize in the classroom is the first one listed above: "Explain by telling how and why." This norm is important in a science class because clear procedural explanation is a highly valued scientific genre. If another person is going to attempt to replicate an experiment, they must have a good understanding of how you got your results.

Maria, as a strong high-status student, struggled with this norm. Once she decided to join in with her group, she would often try to take over and do all the work herself. Maria had to learn to listen to other children's questions and then respond by describing how to do a task, instead of doing everything for the child who was asking for assistance. With time and practice she became a patient and competent explainer, as a result of her observing the norms that have been established in the classroom.

Some Ways to Develop Learning Communities That Support Scientific Habits of Mind

Creating classrooms with shared values that respect and nurture good thinking is a yearlong practice for Caryn, Patty, and their students. More

2–4 Sonja's journal: "I don't understand." "I'll help you."

than anything else, the total culture of a classroom becomes a context for nurturing scientific habits of mind. Thoughtfulness (encompassing knowledge, skills, and dispositions) is a primary attribute: establishing classroom norms through skillbuilding activities; setting the stage for questioning; modeling curiosity, openness to new ideas and skepticism; setting high expectations; and valuing mistakes.

Norms as Part of the Classroom Culture

As Patty related in her story about Maria and herself, establishing classroom norms is extremely important for collaborative experiences to be successful, both from the standpoint of classroom management and shared values that foster scientific habits of mind. Practicing these norms can lay the foundation for lifelong attitudes toward collaboration where children will respect each other and value others' points of view.

Caryn and Patty introduce norms by using skillbuilding activities. Skillbuilders are cooperative games that can be found in many cooperative learning books. We are going to give an example of one that we use, "Master Designer," taken from Elizabeth Cohen's book *Designing Groupwork* (1994). To play Master Designer, children work in groups. Each student gets a set of geometric shapes, and an oak tag folder behind which to manipulate them. One child in each group plays the role of "master designer" who uses some or all of the shapes to make a design. Because the master designer has a folder in front of what she is making, the other group members can't see the design, so they have to ask questions about it. The master designer must give the others directions to replicate the design but cannot show or do it for them. The norm that is most important here is the one that Patty just discussed, "Explain by telling how." If a group member thinks that she has the same design, the master designer checks it to see if there is a match. If successful, that person then helps the master designer explain to others, thus introducing another norm, "Everybody helps."

Caryn and Patty clearly explain how to play these games, but they don't tell the children why they are playing them until after they have had the experience. A follow-up discussion is held where the teachers ask the children to talk about what happened during the activity. Students talk about the ways in which certain explanations were helpful to them, often bringing up such things as the importance of details. For instance, if the master designer says "Take the triangle and put it next to the square," it is not as helpful as if she says "Take the small red triangle and put it on the right side of the square, so that it touches and both edges line up." Because they have just done the activity, children appreciate the importance of a good explanation. Thus, skillbuilding games provide concrete experiences in which students can practice and learn about the behaviors that the norms promote. They know whether they were helped by a good explanation or hindered by one that was not precise enough. They know whether someone tried to take their pieces away to replicate the design rather than giving them clear directions about how to make the pattern themselves. Once the children have learned these lessons from the skillbuilding games, Patty and Caryn can refer back to them throughout the year, asking children to remember the norm and its importance. This kind of common experience and open discussion help to make the norm a shared value in the classroom.

From Social Norms to Student Attitudes: Helping Children to Ask Questions

Setting a climate of shared values through the use of social norms is important. It is through repeated exposure to norms that students have an opportunity to take up and try on a new set of attitudes toward cooperation and learning. One of the attitudes that is stressed in *Benchmarks for Science Literacy* is curiosity that is shown by asking questions: "Science education that fosters curiosity and teaches children how to channel that curiosity in productive ways serves both students and society well" (1993, 173). In traditional classrooms, questions are a frequent occurrence, but they are usually the teacher's questions. Caryn and Patty value children's questions, yet they have found that using a prepared curriculum can put a damper on them, even though the curriculum that they use provides rich, open-ended, multiability tasks. When the activities do not arise naturally from what children wonder about, hands-on science lessons can face students with a collection of materials that they must use without having formulated any compelling questions about the topic at hand. There are many different quality science curricula available for teachers to use, and like Patty and Caryn, many or most elementary teachers rely on lessons created by others. This lack of true inquiry can be a problem. The following story by Patty will give insight into a possible solution.

Patty's Story: Joseph's Questions

Each day in my classroom, after orientation, science began with twenty-seven second graders working in groups, talking, planning, and deciding how they were going to complete their tasks. I was curious how second graders might use questions to help guide their group investigations, and if their own questions could lead them to a deeper understanding of science concepts. I was hoping my second graders would begin to see questions as an effective tool to aid them in their discoveries and that their questions can influence their work.

Looking at transcripts of wrap-up discussions from the first year that I taught Complex Instruction, I could see that both the students and I felt comfortable sharing information about groupwork, but I was asking most of the questions. Of course, some children did question the reporter, and I began to see that they were the ones who showed more engagement with the science concepts. They were demonstrating attitudes that can be associated with scientific habits of mind, such as requesting reasons for answers, comparing different points of view, and being persistent about seeking clarification. I wanted to set a tone for wondering so that more children would raise their own questions during wrap-up. I wanted to establish a type of collaboration where the children and I honestly explored *their* questions, not mine. Giving room for all of us to wonder was important to me; good questions were more important than right answers.

During the next year I deliberately made space for children's questions. I explicitly modeled the types of questions that they could ask. As I gave them time to think they began to pose more questions. I was delighted that they were actively asking questions during wrap-up, but I also realized that they were not using their own questions to motivate or guide their inquiry when they were in their groups. Therefore, I decided to use a "science talk" (Gallas 1995) format to take questioning a step further by listing preliminary questions publicly at the very beginning of an insect unit to see if they influenced children's groupwork, talk, and writing.

We brainstormed hundreds of questions about insects. When we started a unit on shapes, we had the same success. However, on the first day of a unit about crystals, the children had little to ask. Why? I felt it could be their lack of awareness about the subject matter. Insects and shapes are both very familiar in their everyday lives. Crystals represented a new area of study and they seemed to have too little knowledge to form reasonable questions. Using this insight, when we started our next science unit, which was about balance and structure, I decided to wait to elicit questions in a formal way. I wanted children to have concrete experience upon which to base their questions, so I waited until they had three days of hands-on work with scales, balances, and building.

Here is a sampling of their questions after that third day:

Why does a structure fall down?

How do you put joints together?

How does a structure know its own weight?

Why do we need to balance a structure?

What is the difference between a structure and a bridge?

What is a perimeter?

Where do shapes come from?

How short does a building get? (I want to know because I already know how high a structure can get.)

How long does it take to build a structure?

We recorded these questions and we talked about the importance of keeping them in mind as groups resumed their activities. Joseph's question that day was "How do you know a structure can't fall?" Three days of working with pins, straws, and tape had illustrated for Joseph the difficulty of stabilizing a structure.

Near the end of our unit, I invited the father of one of my students, an architect, to visit the class. The day before he came, the students and I brainstormed questions to ask him about buildings in the real world. Joseph asked, "Can you predict when a building can fall over or pivot?" Joseph's question shows his persistent curiosity about the stability of structures and some new insights he has gained about problems that might arise.

Joseph, a social child, enjoyed science and the challenge of a group task but often did not participate in group discussions. In some ways, he seemed more engaged with the materials than with the ideas. However, during this unit he began to participate more actively in wrap-up, sharing interesting comments and observations. For example, as we discussed one wobbly building that a group had made, he offered the theory that braces can strengthen a structure. I feel that Joseph's questions helped to make this difference in his participation because he was able to use them as a guide for his inquiry. Because he wondered about and experimented with the issue of stability, he understood that by putting a brace in the middle and keeping the structure straight it would not fall over.

What I found interesting during this unit was how Joseph was wondering and using his questions to guide his learning. He was a more active participant because of his personal investment in what he found out, and this can be seen as a new attitude or disposition toward learning.

Modeling

Modeling is one of the primary ways that children, and all of us, learn. Caryn and Patty are conscious that students are watching them during science, as they are all day. Often, children take their cues from them. Productive modeling may be intentional and carefully planned as when Patty used Sam from *The Trumpet of the Swan* as an example for the children. Modeling may also be a byproduct of the way teachers embody attitudes and behaviors that they foster in their students. Partly intentionally, and partly because they have spent so much time thinking and talking about science, Patty and Caryn model three of the habits of mind that are discussed in *Science for All Americans:* curiosity, openness to new ideas, and skepticism (1990, 173).

Caryn and Patty display their own curiosity when they show genuine interest in what the children are doing, by being good observers, taking detailed notes while groups are working, and asking many genuine questions both during groupwork and in whole-class discussions. Patty and Caryn often begin questions during wrap-up by stating something that they noticed, followed by something that they wonder about. You might think that several years of having children do many of the same activities would decrease the authenticity of the teachers' curiosity about the tasks. However, we have found that even though children perform the same tasks, their approaches are often so different that the teachers never have to feign interest. Each group is distinct enough that there is always something new happening. The teachers' questions become models for the children who, like Joseph, can learn to use personal questions as a way to focus investigation and become true inquirers.

Caryn and Patty show their openness to new ideas in the way that they accept children's theories and pursue information. They know that children hold ideas about the natural world that may be unconventional according to accepted scientific explanations, but make sense based on their own experiences and levels of development. While the teachers are ready to nudge children toward conceptual change when appropriate, they are also ready to entertain and understand their current theories. Children often devise solutions or ask questions that lead to new tracks about which the teachers are themselves not certain. Patty and Caryn become models of openness when they seek answers in books, or ask Goddard's science facilitator or a Clark scientist, or suggest another experiment the class could do to test competing theories. Often they say to their students "Oh, I never thought of it that way," as they ask a child to continue or elaborate on an explanation.

Skepticism is one of the scientific habits of mind that can be difficult to enact in the classroom unless a proper climate is established. You can all imagine certain settings or certain tones of voice that make the question "Why do you say that?" threatening. However, this is a central question in scientific inquiry and one that we want our children to be comfortable with, to ask each other and themselves. Skepticism is an attribute of a "scientific attitude," according to Frederick Aicken (1991) who, in *The Nature of Science,* says that "criticism, of both our own ideas and those who seek to influence us, is not to be avoided but to be positively sought so that the ideas may be scrutinized, tested, and ultimately improved" (125).

Skepticism is nurtured through the teachers' modeling of the kinds of questions that can be asked, especially ones that probe for further thinking. Caryn and Patty both frequently ask "What makes you think that?" or "What is your evidence?" This kind of skepticism is a feature of much scientific communication. According to Driver, "the criterion for acceptance of a scientific theory is that it is scrutinized and approved by the community of scientists" (1983, 4). So too, in the classroom community of second-grade scientists.

When children hear their teachers ask these questions often, in a positive way that challenges another person to think, they also begin to ask each other questions that provoke thought. This modeling is especially important for children to learn productive ways of talking in groups. In some groups such probing can come across as confrontational. When the questioner asks, "How did you get those results?" the person who has been asked may become defensive. However, Patty's and Caryn's frequent "How do you know" questions create a climate for such talk. The teachers model respect for children's thinking because they take all responses seriously. They also demonstrate that they value giving their students time to think by waiting for children to answer and by spending valuable class time on conversations in which thinking can be made public.

Setting High Expectations

High but realistic expectations are an important part of helping children to develop dispositions of thoughtfulness, which enable them to persevere in the face of difficulty, trying their best in spite of whatever obstacles might arise. Throughout the Goddard School students are expected to reach as high as they can and do their very best. This is particularly the case in science, because it is a schoolwide focus. We have already discussed the fact that students are asked to collaborate, to include all group members, to contribute to group reports, and to fulfill a variety of roles on a rotating basis. These are not easy things to do, especially for the seven-year-olds that Caryn and Patty greet on the first day of school. The teachers work hard to set and maintain standards for performance while meeting the needs of individual children for whom some of these behaviors may be more difficult.

The organizational structure of Complex Instruction helps the teachers to reinforce expectations through the classroom norms about cooperation, so that children like Maria are brought into groupwork. Teachers can use specific feedback to give children clear information about when they are successful, or how they might improve. The rotating procedural roles also provide guidelines for both individual and group performance. The following story about a little girl in Caryn's class may help show how expectations about reporting can offer both challenge and support.

Caryn's Story: High Expectations and Lots of Support

One day, right before wrap-up, Tina came to me and whispered that her chest hurt. I immediately sent her to the school nurse as the rest of the class settled down to listen to the science reports. I called for group one's reporter to come forward and begin. Tina was supposed to be the reporter for the day. Rodney volunteered to take her place and did a fine job.

After wrap-up was over, the nurse told me she thought that Tina had a slight anxiety attack and that she experienced heart palpitations because she was nervous about reporting in front of the class. I was surprised because this incident happened in January and Tina had reported before. During her previous turns, she was hesitant, but she did report. When Tina came back to the classroom she was feeling fine and she and I talked privately about her feelings of anxiety.

I was very sympathetic because I knew what she was going through. I always felt anxious when required to do an oral presentation in high school or college, but I also knew that the more practice I had, the easier it became. I told her about my experiences with a bit of exaggeration. I wanted her know that she was not alone in feeling like this. We came to an agreement that when it was her turn to report next she would attempt it and that I would do anything I could to help her through.

When it was her turn to try her hand at reporting once again, she came up willingly and waited patiently for her audience to settle down so she could start. I gave her the signal that she should begin, but she just sat there in the reporter's chair. I was sitting next to her, doing my best to offer encouragement. Her classmates were also very supportive, saying things like, "It's only us" and "Pretend we are not here" and "Make believe everyone is sitting in their underwear." The last one comes from an episode from the syndicated television show *The Brady Bunch*. Tina laughed at this, but still did not seem to be able to find her voice.

After about five minutes of supportive and encouraging words, her classmates became somewhat frustrated. At this point I thought Tina may have been getting a bit overwhelmed and decided to try something else. I told the class that we should all be quiet so that Tina could gather her thoughts. I asked Tina to begin whenever she felt ready. I was practicing "wait time" and it seemed endless. I think that Tina was holding out, hoping that I would let her off the hook, but I was determined to get her through this report. Surprisingly, the audience did not complain and I was proud of their patience. I was also proud when Tina finally leaned over and whispered in my ear that she thought she was ready. She began with the name of her activity and then seemed to relapse into silence. I asked her if it would be easier for her if her audience asked her questions to get her started and she agreed. She answered the questions as best she could, but was unable to offer any information independent of these questions.

For the remainder of the school year Tina did continue to report orally. Each time our "wait time" decreased and she seemed less anxious. Recently I heard a wonderful story about Tina, now a fourth grader. She confidently gave her group's report and, when faced with tough questions from the audience, never hesitated to respond. When she was in my second grade, I wondered if I was right in not letting her give up; her current confidence and ability suggest that she has risen to the challenge.

Valuing Mistakes

One of the shared values that we promote is that mistakes are not something to be avoided, but rather to be learned from. We believe that teaching children to value mistakes is important, especially in a hands-on science environment where they are likely both to make procedural errors and entertain misconceptions. It is also good for them to learn that scientists frequently make incorrect hypotheses and that even established theories can be overturned by new evidence and new ways of thinking.

According to scientist Humphrey Davy, quoted in *The Art of Scientific Investigation* by Beveridge, "The most important of my discoveries have been suggested to me by my failures" (1950, 81).

One of the greatest challenges of an active, hands-on science program that accepts experimentation and error, is that students must give up their notion of one of the most basic rules that sometimes operates in school: Always get the right answer. Frequently, being wrong carries a stigma with it, and this is as true in a class discussion as it is on a test. Making a public mistake can be embarrassing, so children try to avoid the experience—some by playing it safe, others by being silent. We find that even by second grade many have already adopted this notion of schooling and it is something that we must try hard to overcome. Caryn's story about estimation will illustrate this fact.

Caryn's Story: It's Only a Guess!

Every year my second-grade class is involved in many estimation activities. They have experiences in linear, liquid, volume, and weight estimations. They all seem to love guessing, but cannot stand it if their guesses are not right. In fact, they will emphatically deny that they erased guesses on their papers, even though anyone looking can see the dark erasure marks as clear as day. I tell them that I have perfect 20/20 vision, and they still (with very serious faces) insist that they did not erase.

At one point, I had a "Guessing Jar" poster tacked to a wall. Children used it to record their estimates with a dry-erase pen. While my back was turned, some children even tried to change their guesses by licking their fingers so their saliva could easily erase the marker. It got so bad that two years ago a group of competitive boys would argue about who had the closest guess. And each time I announced we were going to do an estimating activity, the boys would look at one another with a dare in their eyes. After the actual measurement was announced, the ones whose estimates were farthest off moaned and groaned as if I just canceled Christmas.

Estimation may seem like a special case because even a good estimate does not have to be the "right" answer, contrary to what Caryn's children think at the beginning of the year. However, it is one aspect of a larger question for teachers: how to make children comfortable with being wrong. We want students to understand that science is a process, not a set of facts, and there may be several productive ways to approach problems. Sometimes these productive routes are only found through trial and error. The process of arriving at a viable, coherent explanation of some phenomenon often requires, in the words of a Goddard student, "that you figure things out from your mistakes."

Asking Authentic Questions and Receiving Honest Responses

Given the fact that even young children have learned that being right is expected in school, how can teachers help students be willing to value or even to discuss their mistakes? One way is very simple: Patty and Caryn model this attitude by openly talking about their own errors, like misspelling a word on the board, or forgetting that the day's schedule has been changed. The best way that we can answer this question, though, is by suggesting that the teachers create a climate of openness to mistakes through asking authentic questions that provoke honest responses. Because of the structure of Complex Instruction, with several groups working on different open-ended tasks, Caryn and Patty cannot know everything that goes on during activity time. Certainly, they are familiar with the tasks and likely outcomes, but the groups can make many decisions along the way that may lead to different results. Therefore, when the teachers ask questions, they are true requests for information. There is an authenticity to their inquiries that the children respond to directly with honest answers. Patty and Caryn, in turn, value their honesty and give them positive feedback about it. Therefore, there is a mutual give-and-take in which students are comfortable, for example, reporting negative results, such as when one reporter, when asked what happened, offered the fact that "nothing happened." Children also freely admit when they did not do something or do not have answers. A feature of wrap-up that is strikingly different from traditional school talk is that students will correct or disagree with their teacher's interpretation, as when Patty or Caryn try to rephrase students' statements in an attempt to understand. For instance, if Patty were to ask for clarification by saying "So you're saying that the left side went down because it weighed more?" the reporter may respond by saying "No, that's not it. It just has more things on it."

On their part, Caryn and Patty make it clear to the students that they do not expect them to have all the answers and that they are more interested in evidence of thinking than in correct responses. Furthermore, they encourage children to talk about problems and mistakes, particularly during wrap-up. In this context it is possible for both the teacher and classmates to provide suggestions and feedback about miscalculations or procedural errors. Often, the group can come to a new and deeper understanding of the content as a result of a variation in an activity that arises from a mistake. Please remember though, that the high expectations that we explained above are still in operation. Patty and Caryn do not expect errors based on carelessness or lack of effort.

3 Dancing on the Table
The Active Cooperative Science Classroom

Mia and Johnny did not work.

How can you get your group working?

Cooperation.

How can you get them to cooperate?

Dance on the table.

That's a last resort. What could you do before you had to dance on the table?

Get their attention.

How?

Talk to them.

—From Matt's dialogue journal

Cooperative learning, in many different forms, is a well established and widely used technique in many schools throughout the United States. We have found, though, that the word *cooperation* is not one that can be taken for granted and that *cooperative learning* involves more than just putting children into groups if it is to realize its potential. Students need time to practice working together in groups and discussing their group interaction, its problems as well as its successes, with their teacher and their classmates. At the primary level, this is a yearlong process that becomes one of the central features of daily classroom life. Learning how to get along, how to share materials and ideas, how to accept and build on each other's suggestions, and how to focus on the common goal of completing their group task is crucial for group and individual achievement.

You may wonder why we devote a whole chapter to a general

3–1 Matt's illustration "Dancing on the Table"

discussion of cooperation in a book about scientific literacy. We feel that it is a must to work through all the kinks of cooperative learning at the same time as we work on science content because if we don't, groups may not productively think, talk, and write science. There are also some practical concerns: The activities that we use in our classrooms can be very messy (like pouring water or salad oil) or even dangerous (like lighting candles or handling ammonia). If the students cannot cooperate there is a much greater chance that the materials will not be handled properly. Also, these materials are extremely inviting, making it much harder for some children to cooperate and share. Sometimes children, like Maria whom you met in the last chapter, just want to keep the "stuff" for themselves, to be the one who gets to manipulate, build, measure, or stir. Therefore, at least with the children that we teach, we have to work harder at cooperation in science than in other areas of the curriculum.

We mention these issues first because, for teachers who are just beginning to implement hands-on science with young children, such practical considerations are often a primary concern. Importantly, though, we have another reason for dwelling on the cooperative aspect of group-work in science, one that has to do with the habits of mind that we outlined in the last chapter and with our definition of scientific literacy. We agree with Palincsar, Anderson, and David (1993) that there are three components of scientific literacy: "(1) the ability to apply scientific knowledge or concepts in principled ways; (2) facility with the language of science that enables the interpretation as well as production of spoken and written text; and (3) given the inherently social nature of scientific activity, collaborative skills that promote constructive social interaction" (645). It is the third component that we emphasize here.

Caryn's Story: The Complexities of Cooperation

The origin of Matt's journal entry, with which this chapter began, is an interesting one. At the beginning of the 1994–1995 school year I frequently had reporters who were not able to deliver satisfactory reports. I expected my students to give a brief summary of what the group did, along with any discoveries or findings that related to their science experience for the day. To my great dismay, most reporters offered very little information at all. Frequently a reporter would begin to summarize for the class and very quickly I could tell that this summary had not been a collaborative effort. This puzzled me because we spent a lot of time preparing for the roles that were to be used during science. The reporter's role, for example, has two main responsibilities: One is to gather the group together to discuss what they had learned and what they would present during wrap-up. The second duty entails speaking in front of the class, relaying this agreed-upon collaborative report to the teacher and students. This prepared report is given before any questioning or discussion starts.

I found their inability to report peculiar since time and time again I had gone over what the reporter's responsibilities were, and time and time again my students could tell me exactly what a reporter was supposed to do. There was even a sign posted on the wall that reporters could refer to if they were not sure. However, all of this careful explanation did not seem to translate into the form of good reports. Finally, the frustration caught up with me, and I had run out of creative ideas. I called my students together for a group discussion, during which they related their difficulties with trying to get their groups together. Evidently the other children were happy to continue working with the materials while the reporter alone tried to decide what to say to the class. I did not want to take the authority back from the groups, so I told them, "I don't care what you do to get your group together; you can dance on the tables if you have to!" I did not mean for the children to take this literally, but you can imagine how popular this was with my seven- and eight-year-old students!

Well, during our next science session, I saw most of the reporters standing on their tables, shouting for their groups to get together. As I watched this, I could just imagine my principal walking by, and wondered how I was going to explain why these children were dancing and shouting from the tabletops. Although I didn't want the children doing this, it wasn't as dangerous as it sounds because we have sturdy, low tables.

As a class we decided that dancing on the tables was a last resort, and that they could do this only if all else failed. We talked about many strategies that they could use to gather the group together. After that, occasionally a reporter or two would be seen standing on a table trying to get his group's attention. If I saw this I knew that the reporter had exhausted all other avenues and had resorted to "dancing on the table." This problem would be noted and addressed during wrap-up, when the whole class could discuss the issue and brainstorm ways to prevent it from recurring.

The Trials and Tribulations of Learning to Cooperate in the Second Grade

As Matt's dialogue journal entry and Caryn's story indicate, cooperating to complete a joint task like a report is not easy for most second graders. In spite of the difficulty, however, we consider such activities to be an essential part of creating a classroom scientific community. As children gather together to prepare a report, they gain some distance from and perspective about the activity. In thinking about how to make their work public, they move from the "exploratory talk" of groupwork to the "presentational" talk of a report (Barnes 1992). According to Duschl, "When private knowledge becomes public knowledge, a ripple is sent across the scientific landscape" (1990, 78). Thus, the report becomes a way for the entire class to interpret what the group did, to question, connect, and build theories.

As you have seen with Matt's group, though, this is no small task. It is hard work. As children begin to solve scientific problems in second grade, so too do they struggle to find ways to connect with one another and become a community rather than isolated little islands, just at Matt struggled to get his group together to prepare their report.

Structuring Cooperation Through Group Roles

> **We did not learn anything because only the materials manager and the reporter did their jobs.**
>
> *How could your group have gotten things done?*
>
> **Everyone play their roles. Then they will get it done.**
>
> —From Julie's dialogue journal

There are numerous reasons why cooperative groups sometimes do not function properly. One reason is that at one time or another children are bound to overlook their roles. It's difficult to blame the students. Having intriguing science materials in front of them must make it easy for them to forget their group responsibilities. However, it is Caryn and Patty's obligation to make sure that the students don't forget. From the teachers' previous experience, they know that groups are more productive when students actively play out their roles. So if the issue of "role neglect" comes to their attention, they bring it up during that day's wrap-up or the next orientation, giving the children a chance to discuss the issue, knowing that talking through the matter helps ensure success in future rotations.

The transcript below is an excerpt from an orientation in Caryn's class. Tanya had suggested that everyone needs to be a "good role player." Matt picks up her cue and elaborates.

MATT: We need to play our roles because we're not going to get anything done if we don't.

CARYN: What happens if the materials manager doesn't play his or her role?

MATT: Then they will be using the materials in different ways than they were supposed to.

CARYN: Inappropriate ways?

MATT: Yeah, and nothing would get done.

CARYN: First of all, if the materials manager didn't play his or her role, no one would have gotten the materials, and you would have nothing to do in front of you.

ANDY: Yeah, they wouldn't get the bag.

CARYN: That's why it's important to be a materials manager. What if the reporter doesn't play his or her role? What would happen? Ross?

ROSS: Then he'll, then him or her, would, they wouldn't be able to say nothin' up there and they wouldn't know nothin'.

CARYN: That's right. What if the cleanup person didn't do his or her role? It wouldn't make for a very happy teacher, I'll tell you that. Anna?

ANNA: Then nothing wouldn't get picked up or cleaned.

CARYN: Um hm. Andy?

ANDY: Then we would have a pigsty room.

CARYN: A pigsty room.

And what a "pigsty room" Caryn had when the cleanup person didn't play her role. As you can see from this conversation, the children knew the rights and responsibilities which were associated with roles. They could also see the consequences of not playing them. Frequent open discussions like this helped Caryn to establish role playing as a shared value in the classroom, but the children still needed many reminders throughout the year.

The following is another excerpt of transcript about role neglect in Caryn's classroom. This one revolves around the role of checker, whose responsibilities include making sure names are on papers, making sure everyone has filled out the worksheets that help them to record their data, and collecting the papers at the end of the science session. This transcript was excerpted from a lesson that occurred in May, nine months into the school year. In this case Ross, the reporter, has just admitted to Caryn that no one in his group completed a worksheet.

CARYN: Whose job is that though?

ROSS: Rodney's.

CARYN: The checker. Did you play your role?

RODNEY: No.

CARYN: No. So now I get four or five blank worksheets. Right?

RODNEY: Yeah.

CARYN: And do I want five blank worksheets?

RODNEY: No.

CARYN: What do I want?

RODNEY: Five filled-out worksheets.

Caryn was very frustrated with this group because it was May and on this day they were still struggling with assuming their roles. She thought that this was going to be the only trouble spot for the day until Anna raised her hand to say "Actually Miss McCrohon you have nine of them because our group didn't do them either." Caryn reports that she had to remind herself that patience is a virtue, in order to keep her dissatisfaction to herself. She also realized that she would be able to discuss this role neglect issue during the next day's orientation. Besides, the next reporter was going to be Andy, a child who always took his roles seriously, and loved to talk about science. And, after all, the point of wrap-up is to discuss science. Caryn was more than ready for an engaging scientific conversation with Andy. She called him to come up to the reporter's chair. Once settled, he began: "O.K. Well, in our group we really didn't get anything done." At this point Caryn was flabbergasted. She is rarely at a loss for words with her students, but she just sat there listening to Andy explain that the main reason for not accomplishing anything was that most people in the group didn't play their roles. Needless to say, Caryn knew that they had a lot to discuss during their next orientation. Although this kind of day can and will happen at any time, thankfully, it is not typical.

Improving Cooperation Through Student Reflections

Often when working in groups, children run into trouble getting tasks completed because of problems like the role neglect described above. In order for groups to perform successfully, children must have many opportunities to understand the shared values of the classroom and the best way for teachers to help them achieve this understanding is giving them a venue to reflect on group performance. In Caryn's and Patty's classes this is done both orally, during orientation and wrap-up, and in a written format in dialogue journals.

When wrap-up is over, children write in their science journals about what they learned that day. They have the freedom to write about any aspect they choose. After their entries are complete, they go to Patty and Caryn for what they call "challenge questions." At this point, the teachers begin a written dialogue with their students about their science experiences.

Caryn initiated the use of dialogue journals in science. She chose this type of journal for numerous reasons, but primarily for assessment purposes because she wanted a way to document what her students were learning. Sometimes, however, the dialogue does not center around the science concepts of the unit; it revolves around group interaction. The following two examples are taken from dialogue journals. The first is from Ross' journal about an activity involving balance and structure:

> In my group we had to balance straws on two pieces of wood. And we did better than the first day.
>
> *What did you learn?*
>
> I learned that I can't work by myself.
>
> *Can you tell me why it's easier to work with a group?*
>
> It is better to work with a group because you will get your work done.
>
> *What about helping?*
>
> If you help your group then you will get your work done.

As you can see there is not much talk about science, other than Ross' explanation that his group had to balance straws on two pieces of wood. When Caryn asks her first question, she is hoping Ross will answer by telling what he learned about balance. However, Ross focuses on interaction in his group. From experience, Caryn has learned not to force the issue and push for information about science concepts unless she is absolutely sure that the child has something scientific to write about. Caryn suspects that when Ross writes "you will get your work done," he probably means the procedural work of the group, placing a pin in a straw so that the straw will balance. However, she also knows that group collaboration will lead to shared intellectual work. Therefore, she feels that children's reflections on group interaction are very valuable to her students, and in the long run help future groups function better, which in turn will lead to more productive science talk and writing.

In the following example, Carlo reveals the frustration he felt during an activity that involved building a structure. He too has realized some important information that will help him work more efficiently next time, although, again, the realization is not directly related to science:

Structure is when you make a building or a house or a tall thing. Justin was making a house but Katerina wanted to make a square at the bottom and we didn't get anything done because we didn't make up our mind. So the time we started was the time to clean up. We learned that we should draw it before making something, and it was hard because we didn't make up our minds.

Why do you think it is a good idea to design something first?

It's better to design something so you know what you are making.

Even though Carlo's group did not accomplish their assigned activity, he expressed an important insight about the value of planning and it is this that Caryn picks up on in her questions. During the following days after this entry was written, this group had great success. They had learned a valuable lesson from this experience. Allowing the children to honestly express their feelings and frustrations in writing helps them sort everything out. Notice that Carlo did not accuse anyone in particular; instead he placed blame on the whole group by using the word "we" several times. He even tells Caryn that he "learned that we should cooperate in the group." When Caryn reflects on this particular entry she is gratified by how much Carlo has matured. Had he written this at the beginning of the school year, Carlo would most likely have placed the blame on other children. He certainly would not have accepted any of the responsibility for himself. Caryn attributes Carlo's development to the fact that her students, throughout the year, have opportunities to internalize shared classroom values by discussing group problems and solutions orally and in writing.

From Tribulation to Triumph: When Cooperation Works

In the next section of the chapter we will continue to discuss strategies that Caryn and Patty use to facilitate cooperation among their students, this time with an emphasis on the triumphs. It is very rewarding on these days when children work together in a way that almost makes the process seem easy. As you can tell from our discussion of the trials in the previous section, it is *not* always easy. We try to appreciate and celebrate these successes because this is what we support students to work toward.

Communication as a Key Factor in Cooperation

As we have already said, it is important for children to reflect on their group process and role-taking when things fall apart. Teachers almost always hear about it when things go wrong in a group because the

3–2 Cooperation works when everyone's involved

children talk and write about their problems. However, when groups work well together, they often do not comment on the social process because it seems invisible, so the teachers make it a point to. In order to firmly establish shared values in the classroom, Patty and Caryn feel that it is also vital to let their students know when they are doing things well.

Communication is an essential factor if groups are to work together successfully. It requires that children be good listeners so that they can take the ideas, contributions, and needs of others into account. Caryn and Patty sometimes joke that their students have mastered the talking aspect of communication, but need to practice the listening aspect. Children need to be taught ways to communicate with each other, and one way to teach them is by noting and celebrating when they are successful so that they will know what they have done. For this reason, Patty and Caryn always try to point out to their students when good communication has taken place. The teachers find that when students who are having trouble cooperating hear specific feedback about others who are more successful, they often change their behavior in the future because they have a better understanding of the right thing to do.

In the following excerpt from a wrap-up, Caryn is giving a group specific feedback about their successful communication:

CARYN: Let me tell you what I saw in this group. I saw that Mark was a good explainer, and that's on our chart. Andrew asked you for help, which was his right to ask for, right? And Matt helped him, which was his duty. His duty also helped Carrie explain why two hundred centimeters went after one hundred ninety centimeters. Carrie had an answer written down, but she couldn't explain to me why she put two hundred down. Matt explained and she understood. Then Carrie was able to take the information that Matt explained to her, and explain it to Ramone.

ALYCIA: Sounds like Matt did a lot.

CARYN: Right Ramone? So now, not only were Matt and Tina the only two that understood. Now, Andrew understood, Carrie understood, and Carrie understood enough to explain it to someone else. So now all five group members knew the information and why to put it there. That's good cooperation and communication.

There are several notable details about Caryn's observations. First, she is referring to a multiple abilities chart that the class has constructed together, establishing the shared value of being a "good explainer." Second, she is explicit in letting the whole class know that this group followed through in carrying out two critical classroom norms about asking for and receiving assistance. Last, she discusses the consequences of these behaviors, namely the outcome of "good cooperation and communication." Since she has laid the groundwork for shared values, she is able to remind the class about what this successful group did and why it is important. When giving students specific feedback Caryn and Patty use their observations to give concrete, authentic examples that the children can relate to, something they have experienced themselves. It is not as meaningful if artificial situations are used to promote discussions with young children. Even though the teachers work with the norms through skillbuilding activities early in the year (as described in Chapter 2), to some extent norms are still abstract rules until children encounter them firsthand as they are working on science activities. Once children have the experience of enacting (or neglecting) the norms, they have personal detailed information that helps them talk and write about them. Patty and Caryn can refer back to the experiences that children have had with the skillbuilders as a reminder about cooperative behaviors. Similarly, they can ask the class to remember their concrete successes and failures with carrying them out during groupwork.

When we described Complex Instruction, we mentioned the fact that there is conceptual redundancy within each Complex Instruction unit. This design feature is helpful for many reasons: Most importantly, it gives students an opportunity to learn about the major science concepts several different ways. Remember that, on any given day, each group is doing a different activity surrounding the same "big idea." They then rotate through all the activities in the unit. If children do not understand the concept during the first rotation, they have the opportunity to do four or five related activities, and to experience four or five more orientations and wrap-ups from which they can gain the knowledge they need in order to build an understanding of the concept.

In addition to this conceptual redundancy, there is something that we call "procedural redundancy" that is facilitated during wrap-up. Because each reporter describes a different activity, which every group will eventually experience, at times reporters may give advice to groups that have yet to do that task. The excerpt of a transcript below is an example of this type of communication. The children have just finished an activity in which they had to cut ten straws into ten centimeter lengths and thread them together to make a meter stick. They were then supposed to use this flexible device that they created to measure objects around the classroom. As this excerpt begins, Mark has just finished his report about what his group measured and how accurate their homemade meter stick was. He is now fielding questions from his audience:

MARK: Matt?

MATT: Did you use my advice and just make one?

MARK: Yeah.

MATT: Good job.

MARK: Yeah, we were gonna make two but . . .

CARYN: You know what, that makes me happy because that means that people were listening during wrap-up when Matt said that they weren't able to get anything done because they all decided to make their own and it would be easier just to make one. And because of that advice, Matt, both groups after you were able to get one done.

The event that led up to this advice was very frustrating for the members of Matt's group. Each activity that we use is designed so that the children must share materials and work interdependently. However, for some reason, this group had enough straws and strings so they could each make their own meter stick. Even though Caryn made many suggestions about sharing while they were working, the group broke up and they all worked on their own projects. If they had collaborated on a group product, they could have been successful, but time ran out. No one in the group had even finished a meter stick, let alone measured anything. Their lack of success led Matt to advise his classmates who had yet to do the activity to work together to make a single meter stick. That advice enabled the groups that followed to successfully complete the activity and to make interesting discoveries about their flexible measuring tool.

This example also illustrates the value of the rotating activity structure because the sequence of having different groups move through different tasks creates the opportunity for replication, an important process in the scientific community. Both procedural and conceptual insights gained across days can be incorporated into groupwork because children have the chance to benefit from the ideas of others.

Cooperation and the Issue of Status

It's generally accepted by educators that cooperative learning leads to learning gains. But Elizabeth Cohen, designer of Complex Instruction, wanted to know who was learning and when. As a sociologist, she researched what went on inside cooperative learning groups. What she found was very disturbing. Certain children tended to dominate the groups, and they were the ones who were learning the most. To put it simply, the students of high status tend to be more active in groups, and the students of low status, most of the time, participate less. Essentially this discrepancy results in unequal access to learning (Cohen 1994).

Academic status is a major issue even at the primary level, and is especially played out in group dynamic situations. For the most part, if a child is considered to be capable in the areas of reading and math, this view is generalized into an impression of overall intelligence. When these same children enter into a group task in other curricular areas, even if the task does not require reading and math, they will still dominate the group. Other status characteristics mirror the society in which we live and, whether we like it or not, include socioeconomic background, gender, race, ethnicity, religion, language ability, popularity, and appearance.

In spite of growing criticism (e.g., Gould 1981), ever since Binet invented the IQ test, which measures intelligence very narrowly, society has had a one dimensional view of what it means to be smart. However, theorists like Howard Gardner (1983) and Elizabeth Cohen (1994) view intelligence more broadly. Gardner notes the narrow focus that schools place on certain kinds of abilities while ignoring others that are equally as relevant for working inside and outside of the classroom. Gardner's concept of multiple intelligences and Cohen's idea of multiple abilities both recognize that there are numerous ways a person can be intelligent, besides linguistic and mathematical ability. Through reading and studying people like Cohen and Gardner, Caryn and Patty became aware of multiple abilities and also of ways to help solve the problem of unequal access to learning.

Two effective ways to combat status issues in the classroom are part of the Complex Instruction approach. The first is called the "multiple abilities treatment." It begins when teachers explicitly point out to students all the ways there are to be smart besides reading, writing, and math. A teacher can do this using classroom tasks that call for multiple abilities, carefully examining the activities, and looking for all the relevant skills and abilities that will be needed in order for the tasks to be completed successfully. Next, she can publicly tell students what these abilities are. Caryn and Patty write abilities on a chart as a public document that can be viewed and added to throughout the duration of a unit, and referred to as you heard when Caryn gave specific feedback to Mark. When conducting an orientation, the teachers remind children of the abilities needed to complete the activities, and solicit ideas from the class to add to the chart. For example, the list may include such things as accurate measuring, manipulation of small objects, constructing skills, and planning skills. Finally, teachers often repeat the norm that we call the Golden Rule of Complex Instruction: "No one has all of the abilities, but everyone has some of the abilities." They also stress the norm that "No one is as smart as all of us together." This explicit talk about abilities helps to set the stage for the idea that no one child should dominate the group and that everyone can make a valuable contribution.

Caryn's Story: Ross the Measurer and Manipulator

This focus on children's multiple abilities is one of the reasons why I use cooperative learning as a way of teaching science in my classroom. If I were to teach out of a textbook, without the benefit of hands-on activities that require different abilities, the children in my classes probably would not have opportunities to see each other as having these abilities at all. Textbook science involves a good deal of reading, and reading was particularly difficult for Ross, whose story I'm about to relate. Well-designed multiple-ability cooperative learning activities, on the other hand, provide a venue where children like Ross can offer abilities that do not require proficiency in the highly valued areas of reading and math, but nonetheless are important for successful groupwork. Additionally, children like Ross need to be able to see that others value what they can offer to a group. Ross may not have even recognized that he had any important skills to begin with.

In the following excerpt from a wrap-up, Luke, the reporter from Ross' group, is talking about their activity which involved shapes and measurement.

LUKE: Ross, he said today was the hardest group we've ever done so far.

CARYN: Really, did he tell you why?

LUKE: Cuz we messed up four times. The lines . . . we hadda stop. It was hard to draw the lines down that were all straight and every-thing.

CARYN: Well you know what, it was very hard, because you needed an accurate measurer. An accurate measurer. Was anyone in your group someone you could consider an accurate measurer?

LUKE: Ross.

CARYN: Ross? So, Ross, if someone needs to turn to someone and needs accurate measuring, they could turn to Ross then. You seem to be an expert in your group on measuring.

CHILD: I know.

CLASS: And a manipulator.

CARYN: He's also a good manipulator.

CHILD: And he's good at sewing.

CARYN: And he's good at threading needles. Ross, you are just a scientist, I guess, that has a lot of abilities that can help in science group.

LUKE: He don't think he does it good either.

CARYN: I know he doesn't think he does it good and that's why we tell him every day that he does.

Here, Luke notes that it was Ross' measuring ability that helped the group to get their work accomplished. You can see from this transcript that the children were aware of Ross' low self-image which might have resulted from his difficulty with reading. However, they obviously did not agree with his general attitude about himself. Instead, they offered him a great deal of support by pointing out things that he could do well. In my eyes and the eyes of the other students, Ross was someone to turn to when you needed help in math and science, since many of the manipulative activities rely on fine motor control and careful measuring. He seemed to be the only one who did not feel that way.

On this same day, after wrap-up, I gave the students time to work in their dialogue journals. Take a look at what Ross wrote:

I learned that we don't always guess right.

Do guesses have to be right?

No.

What else did you learn?

I learned that I could be a measurer.

The last line of Ross' journal where he stated "I learned that I could be a measurer," leads me to believe that Ross has recognized an ability that he had, after his classmates and I pointed it out to him. What Ross did not realize, though everyone else did, was that he had been an accurate measurer since the beginning of the year. This discussion took place in March, so it had taken Ross seven months to see himself in that light. But it had finally happened, and what is significant is that recognition came from his peers as well as from me. It's important for students to hear these things from teachers, but it is perhaps even more meaningful to hear it from classmates and friends because group affirmation signals that recognizing diverse abilities has become a shared value in the class. With repeated exposure to this shared value, Ross has developed the attitude that he is someone who can do science because he is "a measurer."

This discussion was not unique. My class had frequent conversations about Ross' abilities. One day a set of necklaces made of yarn got very tangled and some of the children were struggling to pull them apart. A suggestion was made that they "give it to the manipulator in the class" and the students automatically gave the tangled mess to Ross because they came to believe that he was our resident expert when it came to such matters. On another day, students were responding to a question that I had posed about what kinds of abilities were necessary to complete a given task. Jake suggested that a good manipulator would be helpful. Without hesitating, another child yelled out "we already have one," meaning that Ross was a good manipulator and that maybe having just one was all our classroom needed.

Ross was not the only child in the class who did not think of himself as "smart." Mia had a similar view of herself. However, there was a big difference between Ross and Mia. Ross never gave up; he always put forth a one hundred percent effort. Mia, on the other hand, often gave up easily when faced with a challenge, or got one of her mystery sicknesses, hoping she could avoid doing an activity. Maybe this is why, as you will see, Mia did not get the same kind of spontaneous support that Ross got from classmates.

Below is a story about Mia and her group that is written by Maureen. She constructed it from the field notes she took on a day while observing in Caryn's class. Mia's group was supposed to be working together to construct a sturdy structure out of straws.

Maureen's Story: Mia's Great Discovery

Four children were in a group building with straws. Their task was to figure out what materials were best for making a structure sturdy, choosing from tape, pins, wire, or clay to fasten the joints. The facilitator assigned everyone the job of making squares, some with tape, some with pins. As they began to work, they decided that they would put their squares together to make a base first. By this point, the children were all working diligently, each one making a square that held together quite well, all except for Mia. Her square kept collapsing because she couldn't get the pins to stick at an angle. She kept having to start over. She picked up her lopsided square and put it next to the other children's, seemed to compare them and said, "I'm just kidding." At this point, Mia switched to tape but still couldn't join the two straws when they were placed perpendicular to each other. After several more failed attempts, she took a straw and folded it about an inch from the end, making an "L" shape. She took another and did the same. Then she joined the two so that they overlapped and she could tape the overlapping portion.

Each of the other children had constructed several squares by this time and the facilitator was attaching them to make a large structure. Mia was pretty much excluded from the activity because she had no square to contribute, but she kept working on her own. After she made her square she handed it to the facilitator to add to their structure. Hers was much smaller than the others because of the folded ends and it didn't fit. When her square was rejected, she said to nobody in particular, "They don't like how I do my squares." Another little girl told her that she put too much tape on it, to which she replied "I can't do nothin'." I would like to think that the facilitator felt sorry for Mia at that point. For whatever reason he then suggested that they use Mia's square as a window because it fit inside the two larger squares. Hearing this, she declared that if it was going to be a window it would need a cross on it, so she took it back and put a straw diagonally across, which acted like a cross brace. Mia was trying to make a decoration, but she discovered an important structural component. Her square was the only one that easily accommodated a cross brace because of its smaller size. Caryn was unaware of my observations as the wrap-up began:

CARYN: OK, I have something to say about this. Mia.

MIA: Yes.

CARYN: Brilliant idea. Brilliant idea. Do you understand what this is? This cross right here braces it from the sides.

CHILD: And it's a door.

CARYN: And it braces it from the top. This is a cross brace . . . like beams. Mia this is an important discovery that you made.

MIA: I did it because um I . . . I . . . I made crosses on every window that I made cuz it . . . it . . . it just reminds me of God. I put a cross.

CARYN: OK, but this is an "X." And what I'm telling you Mia is that this cross or cross beam does not look like a cross, but an "X" . . . is making the sides and top very sturdy, very sturdy. This window is not going to collapse easily. Look right here. This side right here would collapse, see this collapse? *(Demonstrates with another square)* See the collapse that's happening right here? Let's try it with Mia's window. *(Pushes on the structure)* Is it collapsing?

CHILD: No.

CHILD: Put all your might into it.

CARYN: I'm putting just as much might as I did to this. Do you see what this cross beam did? That made it very sturdy. Mia what an amazing discovery.

Here, Caryn is beginning to publicly assign competence to Mia, meaning that she is pointing out exactly what Mia did and why it was important to her group. She is purposely doing this so every child will hear something about Mia's contribution to the group's success, hoping that it may help raise Mia's status among her peers and give her something to feel good about. Caryn and Patty try to "assign competence" to low-status children whenever possible. However, as in the case of specific feedback, teachers must base their comments on authentic observations. If they are not honest in describing what they have seen, children will simply not value what a teacher says when it comes to such issues.

As the discussion goes on, we can see that the children themselves understand the value of Mia's discovery. The transcript continues with Ramone saying something that surprised Caryn:

RAMONE: I think Mia should take that home.

CARYN: I think Mia should get two thumbs up for her ingenious decision. Excellent. Ramone?

RAMONE: I think Mia should bring that home because she just found a discovery that we might not have found.

CARYN: Yeah, Mia has a wonderful ability to . . . I guess we'll call it a builder and designer.

RAMONE: Or a finder.

CARYN: Or a discoverer even, yes Ramone. Excellent. Excellent.

Normally, group projects stay in the classroom because all the children want to take them home. What surprised Caryn about this is the fact that Ramone thinks that this discovery is so important that Mia deserves the honor of taking the structure home. By now Mia is beaming with pride with her new found fame. By naming her ability as "builder" or "designer," Caryn is hoping that this fame might follow her to other activities that call for similar skills and that her classmates will be more likely to include her as a potentially valuable group member. In fact, Mia was "famous" throughout the rest of the unit. The crossbrace became known as "Mia's discovery," and was referred to as that each time it came up during groupwork or wrap-up. Ultimately her fame lasted even longer than the structure unit itself. A few months later while working on an extension activity dealing with structural issues, Andy, a high-status, high-achieving child, stated to his group, "We should use the thing that Mia discovered."

Interdependence and Abilities: Cooperative Group Talk

One focus of the next story is this strategy of giving students limited materials to complete the task so that they are required to work as a team in order to get their activity done. The other focus, though, is the different abilities of the children, and how they came to value the work of one member who was not a high-status child.

Patty's Story: Manuel's Sturdy Base

Manuel entered my second-grade classroom in a quiet way, listening carefully to directions. He caught my attention immediately because it was easy to see he was shy and wanted to please his teacher. Manuel had come from New York City and was a transition bilingual student, meaning that he had received instruction in both Spanish and English prior to coming to my class. Manuel was a gentle, friendly child and was interested in his classmates. He seemed to enjoy science and was a determined group member, always carefully considering how to solve a problem. When he was sharing his ideas, I would often have to ask him to repeat himself because his voice did not carry in our large, echo-filled room. He would do so, but reluctantly, as he was afraid of mispronouncing a word or misunderstanding the question he was asked. Often, Manuel preferred to demonstrate how to do something rather than explaining it orally.

When Tara, the reporter in Manuel's group, presented their report about a bridge-building activity, a student in the audience asked her how her group built their structure. Tara replied simply, "We just put it all together." From this response, you would probably think that Tara, Manuel, Sarah, and Aaron built their structure with relative ease and cooperation. However, an examination of the actual process reveals something quite different. Below is an excerpt from their taped conversation during groupwork.

TARA: Hey I'm gonna make my own thing. I'm makin' my own thing.

MANUEL: Yeah that's what I'm doin'.

TARA: I'm makin' a bridge. I'm makin' a bridge.

MANUEL: I'm makin' a house. I'm makin' a house.

At this point all of the children are working separately. Each one is beginning to cut and tape straws together to make a structure. Tara says that she is making a bridge. Manuel says that he is making a house. Given his limited experience with English, Manuel may have been using the task card differently. He probably had to rely more heavily on the illustrations than on the printed directions. His description of what he is doing fits much better with what was actually depicted on the activity card than with what the words said. Next, a classroom visitor asks them to read the instructions because she has noticed that the group may be "on the wrong track." Aaron reads, "Use twenty straws to build a structure." It then becomes clear that the group has a total of twenty straws *between them* to complete this activity. Several minutes go by and the discussion continues about the objects they are making and the need for scissors, tape, and more straws. Then Manuel makes a suggestion:

MANUEL: Hey guys, let's work as a team.

AARON: Guys, let's work as . . .

MANUEL: We work better as a team.

TARA: How about if we stick all these together [meaning the straws].

AARON: No way!

Although Manuel has suggested cooperation, his proposal meets with resistance when Aaron realizes that "working as a team" means joining his straws with those of the other children. Then, the children decide that their problem will be solved with additional supplies. Tara, the facilitator, is sent to try again to get more straws. With the help of Patty's student teacher, Heidi Miller, they finally realize that they cannot use more than twenty straws. Tara returns to the group with the bad news:

TARA: I asked if we could get more straws. She said we can't.

SARAH: That's it? We don't get any more straws?

TARA: No.

Then Aaron, who was reluctant before, resubmits the idea of putting all of their straws together:

AARON: Hey, I've got a great idea. Why don't we take off our straws and put them on Manuel's?

SARAH: Why? No way.

TARA: No way.

MANUEL: I'm doing the house you're doing. Hey we're supposed to do that *(Points to the picture on the activity card).*

Now it is Tara who rejects this idea and the conversation briefly degenerates into second-grade name calling. It isn't long, however, before Aaron acts on his own suggestion and begins to add his straws to Manuel's structure because it is sturdy and looks like the base of the building depicted on the activity card. Heidi, the student teacher, revisits the group to make certain that they are on task:

HEIDI: Do you all understand why there are only twenty straws?

SARAH: No, I don't.

HEIDI: You don't understand why there are only twenty straws? Well let's look at this *(Brings over the card and begins to read).* Build one structure. So, do you understand?

SARAH: Yeah.

HEIDI: Build one structure.

SARAH: Yeah.

HEIDI: Manuel, do you understand now about twenty straws and what your group is doing?

MANUEL: Yeah, we're taking it off.

TARA: Hey look what I'm doing.

HEIDI: OK, so you're building one structure with the group.

TARA: Yeah. I'm cutting these so I can give them to Aaron. Aaron I broke your thing.

SARAH: Look it Manuel, I'm gonna put my, look it Manuel.

TARA: Look it, she's snipping hers already.

MANUEL: To put it on mine.

Once Heidi reiterates that the students would not be given extra materials to complete their task, they finally begin to realize that it will be necessary for them to work as a team instead of individually. All of the children then begin to work together to build onto Manuel's straws. They choose

Manuel's structure as a base because it provides the strongest foundation. It is clear that Manuel was able to use the picture on the card to direct his construction of a very firm and sturdy base.

While Aaron takes his own structure apart and begins working closely with Manuel to build a single structure, he encourages the two girls to do the same. Tara then removes the pins from her straws and the conversation continues:

TARA: Do you want me to help you?

MANUEL: Yeah, come over to this side. I need more straws, more straws. I need more straws.

TARA: Stick it like that.

MANUEL: I need one more straw, then it's finished.

TARA: We're not finished yet.

A careful examination of the actual group process demonstrates that these students did not just simply cooperate and quickly put together their group structure, as one might assume from Tara's statement during her report that they "just put it all together." In fact, we can see that they struggled in their attempts to get the activity done at first because they were all working in a parallel manner to put together their own structures. It was not until Heidi emphasized that they could only use twenty straws that the children began taking apart their separate structures and placing the straws on Manuel's base.

In this example there are many points of interest. Manuel, as a transition bilingual student, was not a high-status child within the classroom. Although he was well-liked, he was shy and reading was difficult for him. In this example, though, it was his ability to use information from the illustration to guide him in designing his base that made him a valuable group member. Patty did not have access to this information about Manuel on the spot or she could have "assigned competence" to him by pointing out that his ability to interpret a diagram helped his group to design a better building. Nevertheless, the children themselves showed that they recognized his skill because they used his base. Acknowledging the importance of many abilities, not just reading and math, as well as giving students limited materials fostered group interdependence and a level of cooperation that would not have occurred otherwise.

Understanding how to cooperate in groups is a continual process. The longer children are in situations that require them to work together, the easier it becomes for them. Children tend to triumph after the trials because of the concrete experiences that these difficulties offer. However,

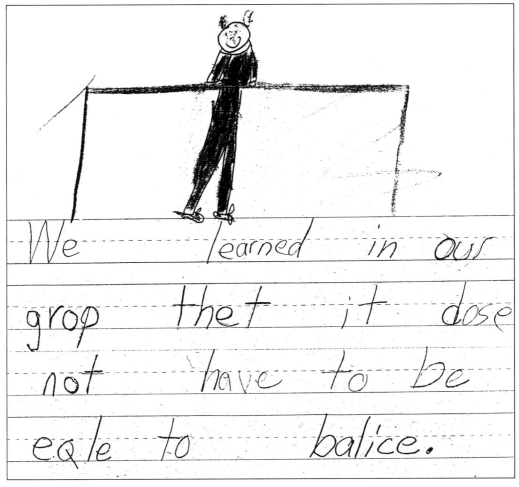

We learned in our grop thet it dose not have to be eqle to balice.

3–3 Julie's dialogue journal

it is not just the experiences themselves that make a difference. The real triumphs happen because Patty and Caryn take time to talk about difficult situations and find solutions with the class, and similarly discuss the successes that children achieve. Some of these successes can be celebrated by children like Ross, Mia, and Manuel, who may have been excluded in a more traditional approach. Both the experiences and repeated whole-class discussions establish cooperative roles and norms, first as shared values and then as student attitudes that represent scientific habits of mind.

In the journal entry that began this chapter, Matt wrote about "dancing on the table." It was his way of explaining a trying situation, the frustration that reporters have when attempting to gather their groups for discussions. Now we'd like to share a transcript excerpt from Caryn's class later in the year. We think that it speaks for itself and is an interesting contrast to Matt's journal entry. Julie, the reporter, started with a familiar beginning: "I learned that . . ." She was immediately interrupted by Ramone, who was in her group. He rephrased what she had just said: "We *all* learned that . . ." Julie accepted his correction with a smile and continued, "We all learned." Julie had no need to dance on the table.

4 *Science Talk*

Did you discuss this with your group?

—Dina, a second grader

Hands-on science is often thought of as activity based, children doing things—and that is our definition too. However, we have come to realize that encouraging children to talk about what they do is equally important for a number of reasons. As we have already shown in Chapters 2 and 3, we highly value children's conversation in their groups; we want them to talk to each other while they are working on their activities. We have found, though, that a large percentage of this peer talk is procedural or social, both of which are useful in getting the task done and in building a working community. However, children need the help of an adult to acquire the ways of thinking and talking that are valued in school science. They also need to distance themselves from the attractive and engaging materials to really ponder the concepts that underlie the activities.

Patty's Story

Science had set my room abuzz! Looking over my class of twenty-five students, in five groups doing five different activities with all the various materials needed for each sometimes made me dizzy. It was exciting for me to see the earnestness of children working together, yet our hands-on discovery science program forced me to evaluate management issues often, especially during the first year of implementation. In the spring of that year I was faced with a difficult decision about how to use time because some groups worked through their activities more quickly than others. As anyone who has taught second graders knows, they are active and impulsive; when they finish one activity, they need a clear sense of what to do next or else they will find something to do. Some tasks could easily be adapted or repeated; others were not as easily extended. Often,

4–1 A reporter and his group during wrap-up

some groups had to wait while others finished. I did not want them to begin something totally different, since so much was going on in the class anyway. My initial idea was to shorten the activity period, but that felt wrong. Making the analogy to writing or reading time, I wanted the children to have an extended period of *doing* science and worried that decreasing their work time might shortchange their experience. On the down side, it meant that on some days certain groups might not get a chance to finish. On the up side, though, it meant that we could have a longer discussion after the activities were over. But I also worried that our wrap-up conversations would not be as rich if I curtailed the children's observations and experiences. Would they have enough time to work with, consider, and discuss the problem that they were trying to solve? I announced to the children that we would work for a shorter time, thinking that groups would have about twenty minutes instead of their usual half hour. To my delight, I found that this longer discussion was very productive and that cutting back on small group time did not hinder us from having a great talk.

A Description of Wrap-up

As we mentioned in our description of Complex Instruction, small group work in science is bracketed by whole-class meetings, much like a writers' workshop, which starts with a minilesson and ends with sharing time. The beginning meeting, which we call orientation, is teacher-led, and is the time for instruction or demonstrations, tips on using the materials, or reminders about working in groups. This gathering is a signal to children that science is beginning and they know that they will receive information that will be useful to them when they start to work with their classmates.

After they have worked in their groups, they again convene on the rug for a discussion that we call "wrap-up," one that, although teacher-led, is very child-centered. It is teacher-led because Caryn and Patty moderate and often carry on a prolonged conversation with the reporter and group members. However, the discussions always follow the children's topics. The teachers do not use many predetermined questions because they never know what the children will bring up, but they do have an overall goal and ideas about the science concepts that they hope to discuss over the course of a unit.

As you know, each child has a different procedural role during science, one of which is reporter. Wrap-up is the time for that child to tell the rest of the class what the group did. Remember that the group is supposed to work together on their report, but the reporter is responsible for actually telling the class what went on in the activity. Both Patty and Caryn find the rotating reporter role very helpful in distributing the responsibility for talking to the rest of the class. In their urban second grades, there is a wide range of comfort with school talk and an equally wide range of English proficiency. Some children never speak during wrap-up unless they are in the role of reporter. The reporter role is a way to give these children practice at "talking science" and the support that they need to do so.

Since each group does a different activity, at the beginning of a unit there is a need for communicating basic information about what the groups did. This need to know on the part of the audience means that there is an authenticity about wrap-up, with children having real information to contribute. The teachers are also part of the authentic audience, since after visiting with five groups that are doing different open-ended science activities, Caryn and Patty cannot know precisely what went on in any particular group for the whole period. Not only would it be impossible for them to see everything that is happening, but they both feel that excessive monitoring of groups decreases the children's independence and interdependence. So the students know that when the teacher asks a question about what they did, it is an honest request for information.

Supporting Children to Talk About Science

The real challenge for the teacher and the most basic definition of "science talk" at the second-grade level is that the talk be about the science content. Ideally the reporter should begin by telling "what happened," providing a procedural sequence. In reality, children use a number of other beginning strategies. They provide interpersonal information, either talking about problems or pointing out how well they worked together. As we discussed in Chapter 3, when talking about the importance of cooperation, if the story of "what happened" centers on behavioral issues, Patty and Caryn usually acknowledge and ask questions about the group's successes or difficulties. Classroom community dynamics are vital to the success of their science teaching and they both feel that it's important to show children that those aspects of the activity are worth talking about. However, because this is time for talk about the science content, they almost always attempt to then refocus the reporter's attention to telling "what happened" in terms of the science activity, unless a group's problems prevented them from having any results to report.

Although "What happened?" seems like a simple question to an adult, providing a recount is not easy for children, especially at the beginning of the year. The task for the reporter is not to tell a narrative, as they might in sharing time, choosing what they consider to be memorable or reportable. The task in wrap-up is to provide a report that is a factual recount of a science activity. Ochs, Taylor, Rudolph, and Smith (1992) differentiate stories and reports, thus:

> Stories are similar to reports in that both are centered around past-time events and both allow for the possibility that narrators may posit causal explanations or causal links between events. However, stories are unlike reports because stories focus on—and may even be motivated by—a central problematic event or circumstance. (42)

The teachers, though asking "What happened?," a question that could prompt a story, actually hope to hear a recount of the science activity. According to Derewianka (1990), a factual recount usually has the following features:

- It includes the use of third-person pronouns.
- The details are usually selected to help the reader reconstruct the activity or incident accurately.
- Sometimes the ending describes the outcome of the activity, e.g., in a science experiment.
- Mentioning personal feelings is probably not appropriate.
- Details of time, place, and manner may need to be precisely stated.

- Descriptive details may also be required to provide precise information.

- The passive voice may be used.

- It may be appropriate to include explanations and justifications.
  (16)

Obviously, many of these attributes are not characteristic of the language of seven-year-olds, passive voice being the prime example. The second graders almost always speak in the first person, include some affective information and use the active voice, yet some reports come pretty close to this description of the genre.

Let's look at two examples of reports, one from each classroom, that successfully relate what happened in a way that approximates a factual recount. In the first example Asha, the reporter, is describing an activity in which her group diluted apple juice by adding water. Patty gives a minimal prompt, "OK go ahead," and Asha takes this turn:

> When we poured the water into the apple juice and it kinda looked like beer . . . it's gross it did. And then someone put eight spoons . . . four spoons of water in and we tasted it. It tasted pretty strong and then we put four more in and then it tasted weaker and then we put eight in and it tasted weaker and then weaker and weaker and weaker.

After this explanation, Patty evaluates by saying "That's right" and asks no further questions about what happened, but rather goes on to inquire about a graph that the children made to display their results. When Patty and Caryn consider a report to be an acceptable version of what happened, they don't have to prompt any more for the procedural details. Instead, they can follow with questions relating to why such results occurred or what they mean—in this case by thinking about the graph.

In the second example the reporter also fulfills his obligation to tell what happened in one initial turn. Caryn simply says, "Come on up," and Curtis offers the following:

> OK the name of what we were doing was measuring with millimeters. Now what we had to do is draw a picture of each object and write its name in this little square which was very difficult but we managed to do it. Then you hadta guess the length of each object and then write your guesses on it and then measure . . . measure each object to see how long it really is and then we had to put down how much it really is and

then the guess . . . write down how close and find the difference between your guess and the actual length.

After this turn, Caryn asks no additional questions to find out what the group did, but rather begins to inquire about how they computed the differences, asking them to make their thinking explicit.

It's easy to see that Curtis' report contains many features of the genre of factual recount as described by Derewianka (1990). In particular, it includes details to help the listener reconstruct the activity and it tells the manner in which they did it. This report does not tell the outcome of the activity as such because it does not reveal what their answers were. Presumably the answers would differ from group to group because they are derived from children's estimates. So, for this activity, Caryn considered the actual answers less important than the process of finding the differences which Curtis describes very well. Curtis' report differs from Derewianka's description of a procedural recount because he does not use the third person and he evaluates the difficulty of the task (although he tacks it on at the end of a sentence after giving the procedural information). It is important to remember, though, that reports are spoken, not written like the procedural recounts that Derewianka describes, and delivered face-to-face, not to a distant audience. Given the fact that Curtis was seven years old, and was not being explicitly taught the genre of factual recount, we think that this example is quite remarkable.

A transcript example from January shows that, as the year progresses, children begin to internalize the request to tell "what happened" as a recount. Notice the way that Luke begins his report:

> First, I'm gonna say . . . I'm gonna say what we did in the group. The um worksheet says to, like, um, draw a picture of what you're gonna measure and how much you guess and at first we didn't really get that.

Unlike Curtis and Asha, most reporters who tell "what happened" give a partial version of what took place, after which Patty and Caryn ask questions to determine more fully what the group did. Again, it's important to state that these questions are rarely test questions for which the teachers desire one particular answer. Rather, their purpose is to clarify or build on what the reporter offers.

This open-ended questioning frequently results in a very conversational feel to wrap-up, even though it is not true conversation since both teachers have a pedagogic agenda: to focus the discussion on the science content. Wrap-up discussions are similar to what Tharp and Gallimore (1988) call "instructional conversation." They explain, "the concept itself contains a paradox: 'Instruction' and 'conversation' appear contrary, the one implying authority and planning, the other equality and responsiveness. The task of teaching is to resolve this paradox" (111). As part of our analysis of wrap-up transcripts, we have seen Caryn and Patty trying to resolve this paradox through the use of a wide repertoire of teaching strategies.

One of the strategies that you will recognize in the transcripts is the traditional three-part sequence that includes Initiation, Response, and Evaluation (IRE) (Cazden 1988). For instance, if a teacher asks "What is the name of that flower?" and a child responds, "A rose," the teacher will likely say "Very good." This kind of question is often a request for display of knowledge that the teacher already knows rather than an authentic desire to hear what the other person thinks. The third turn, then, evaluates how well the response that's given matches the answer that was expected. In contrast, if two friends are walking in a garden and one asks for the name of a flower, the same response may be met with something like, "Oh I didn't know that there were orange roses." In this case, the person asking would presumably not already know the answer, but rather would truly like to know what the other person thinks. Since it is an authentic question, the response would not be evaluated, but rather accepted or used to continue the conversation.

When we sat down to analyze transcripts, we found that wrap-up often lacks the third evaluating move on the part of the teacher because Patty and Caryn ask questions that do not have single right or wrong answers. Many of Caryn's and Patty's questions are collaborative in the sense that they use questions to coconstruct with the reporter an account of what the group did, at the same time modeling for children the kinds of information that an audience might need. At the beginning of the year, Patty and Caryn ask the reporters many questions to help them tell what happened. However, we have found that over time children begin to expect fuller accounts from their classmates, as evidenced by this example from February:

CAROL: We learned how to um make shapes. Mark said that um he learned how to make shapes, and Tina said she, that she knew . . . she learned how to make them and measure them.

CARYN: Make them and measure them? I think you have some questions here.

ANDY: What group were you in? What did you do in your group besides make shapes? What did you do, "cemetery" group or whatever?

Andy's questions are authentic requests for information, just as many of Caryn's and Patty's are. Since several of the activities involve making shapes, he wants Carol to be more specific. The symmetry (what he called

4–2 Solving a balance scale program

"cemetery") group is in fact quite different from the others, and he honestly doesn't know if that is the group she was in. The teachers have found that, as a result of their constant modeling, more and more children ask questions to elicit information as the year goes on.

An example from later in the year shows that questioning has become a collaborative effort. Rodney has done the balance activity in which his group experimented with placing weights at different points on a balance scale:

RODNEY: *(Long pause)* Hm. OK in our group we um hadda balance something . . . the weights and we hadda balance two on each thing. Like say a ten gram on the same thing. Like say if um. . . .

CARYN: I don't think they know what you mean by thing.

Rodney begins with a very vague description which prompts Caryn to speak for the audience, requesting that he be more specific. She offers to give him the scale to demonstrate. It is a plastic balance arm with ten pegs on each side, numbered from the fulcrum to each end. After a few more turns talking about the scale itself, he begins to explain the activity:

RODNEY: OK say I put this one right here that'd be out. Cuz if it's out it's going down there. Cuz the balance goes down not in . . . down like that.

ALYCIA: Like the higher the number goes . . .

RODNEY: *(Interrupts)* Yeah! The lower it goes [meaning the balance arm].

As Rodney demonstrates by putting one ten-gram weight near the end of the scale, Alycia offers the beginning of a generalization or theory that he is able to complete. His agreement and enthusiasm are marked by both his tone of voice and by the fact that he interrupts her to finish the sentence. The theory that they co-constructed deals with distance, so Caryn begins to question Rodney about the weight:

CARYN: But explain to us. This is ten grams.

RODNEY: Yes.

CARYN: And this is ten grams.

RODNEY: Yes.

CARYN: But you've got the same amount of weight on each side and it's not balanced.

RODNEY: I have it! Because it's on different numbers.

Again, it's apparent that Rodney is constructing knowledge during this discussion by his tone of voice. He is obviously excited when he gets the insight that "different numbers" are important. He is being very concrete by talking about the numbers on the balance arm rather than about the distance, so Caryn continues to probe:

CARYN: What do the numbers have to do with it?

RODNEY: Because if say that I put this one . . . right here it would be even because the numbers are on the even . . . both the same numbers and it'd be even if it wasn't like . . .

CARYN: But what if there weren't numbers there?

RODNEY: Then it'd be these. You'd have to count these [the pegs].

ALYCIA: I'm getting confused.

MARK: Yeah very confused. I'm confused.

As Rodney repositions the weights so that they're the same distance from the fulcrum and thus balance, Alycia voices confusion and Mark agrees with her. When several children start to talk, Caryn articulates the importance of questioning and children begin to raise their hands directing their queries to Rodney:

CARYN: Excuse me wait a minute. If they're confused Rodney, they have to ask you questions.

MARK: So Rodney the higher the number . . . the . . . the lower. . .

RAMONE: *(Interrupts)* So if I put this right here *(Points to peg)* . . . does it weigh more?

RODNEY: Yeah.

MARK: But Rodney hold on. Rodney these . . . these things all weigh the same.

RODNEY: But I put a new gram on it to make it more weight. I was gonna put two of these on this but you see.

MARK: Rodney how do you know it's that many?

RODNEY: I can make it even.

MATT: Rodney what do we count if there's no numbers we don't have X-ray vision I mean we can't . . .

RODNEY: We count these [pegs].

MATT: Oh cuz you pointed over this end like *(Unclear speech)*.

As the dialogue continues, Caryn asks a question that is the conceptual counterpart of the one that she asked before. First, she asked about the same amount of weight not balancing; now she inquires about different amounts of weight balancing:

CARYN: Rodney was there any way that you could have made it equal with um different weights on each side, different amount of weight?

RODNEY: I can make it equal. *(Rodney moves the weights; many children talking)*

RODNEY: It's ah even.

CARYN: Is that even now? Don't touch Ramone. This says ten, twenty, thirty grams. This says ten, twenty, thirty, forty grams. Is it balanced?

CHILDREN: Yeah.

CARYN: So we know . . . we know right now that it doesn't necessarily have to have the same amount of weight does it?

RODNEY: No.

In this discussion, even though Caryn's support was crucial, many of the children also entered into the process of questioning and clarifying. As the year progresses, children anticipate such questions, and often give fuller accounts on their own. Patty and Caryn find that they have to ask fewer and fewer questions to hear an account of "what happened."

After a number of children have become comfortable with giving a sequence of "what happened," the teachers up the ante and request that reporters tell what they learned, not merely what they did. This functions as a good prompt because it challenges many of the children, but yet still allows for multiple points of entry. It can raise the level of talk for those who are ready, but does not prevent others from contributing in their own way. For instance, children may still focus on affect, by saying "I learned that it was hard." Many of the students, though, begin to reflect on the science content or on their own thinking.

Focusing Children's Attention

Another important role for the teachers in these wrap-up discussions is to help the children select a focus of attention. As in many hands-on science classrooms, the activities that Caryn's and Patty's children do are open-ended and uncertain in such a way that groups have to negotiate and make decisions about how to proceed. Consequently, there are multiple variables for children to attend to. When students do these rich, complex activities, they often do not know what to concentrate on. According to Millar and Driver (1987):

> The sheer richness of the observable world means that without a theory to guide observation, we would be incapable of deriving any useful knowledge whatsoever. Without a theory to guide, all manner of distracting and irrelevant data would necessarily be amassed . . . Children's ability to observe involves their learning of a conceptual framework which identifies the elements of a complex situation which are officially "worth observing." Only when the framework has been grasped is the observation possible. (42–43)

In many ways, this quote embodies what is so important about wrap-up and why Patty made the decision that she discussed at the beginning of this chapter. When reporters begin to tell what happened, even if they are constructing a recount, there is often very little selection from among the many facets of the activity. Children often do not know what to pay attention to and, in fact, frequently concentrate on aspects of their experience that are irrelevant or tangential to the science content of the activity. The excerpt that follows is a perfect illustration of this. The children have popped popcorn in a test tube over a candle flame and Caryn is trying to help Rodney, the reporter, to think about how the kernel changed:

CARYN: OK I asked you one more question before you even started. The change of the popcorn before and after you cooked it.

RODNEY: Umm *(Long pause)*.

CARYN: Comparing it. Remember we talked about comparisons? Compare the two popcorns . . . the one before and the one after.

RODNEY: The one before . . . on the side was . . . the first one was burnt.

CARYN: But what about before you even put the kernel of corn into the test tube? What did it look like?

RODNEY: Um it had . . . it already had oil . . . a little oil and popcorn.

CARYN: That's not my question. You took a piece of popcorn out of the box . . . out of the bucket right?

RODNEY: Yes.

CARYN: Before you put it into the test tube what did it look like?

RODNEY: Just a plain old test tube.

Here, the immediate source of confusion seems to be caused by the pronoun "it." A more global cause, however, is what Millar and Driver call "the sheer richness of the observable world." When Caryn asks "What did it look like?" she thinks that it is obvious that she means the popcorn. But it is not obvious to seven-year-old Rodney who found the "plain old test tube" equally worth his interest.

What Caryn is attempting to do here is a strategy often used by both teachers. After listening to the child's account of what happened, Patty and Caryn try to help the reporter to focus on a particular aspect of their group experience by building on what that child offers, and through questioning, to enable the child to state that a certain result occurred. This is what science educator Mary Budd Rowe (1978) calls "choosing relevant properties to pay attention to" (185). With the teacher's support to determine something that is "worth observing," reporters become able to focus on an aspect of the task that then becomes the object of joint attention for further dialogue. Through this dialogue, many children's contributions begin to be more *scientific,* in the sense that they are more focused observations about the science activity.

In the following example, Patty is talking with Lauren about an experiment in which her group cooked a raisin. Children often introduce things that they find to be the dramatic aspects of this activity, especially the fire of the candle flame. In the same way that Caryn was trying to help Rodney make comparisons, Patty is hoping to help Lauren to talk about the change in the raisin, which is the point of the experiment:

PATTY: The raisin people got their raisins cooked like yesterday. Were there different tastes for the raisins? The cooked raisin and the uncooked raisin?

LAUREN: I tried it.

PATTY: Was it different?

LAUREN: Yes it was a LOT different.

PATTY: How was it a lot different?

LAUREN: Cuz the real raisin tasted good and the other one didn't. It tasted too yuk cuz it was mushy.

By asking "Was it different?" Patty successfully helps Lauren to make the comparison between the raw (what Lauren calls the "real raisin") and the cooked. Although Patty's question seems as though it asks for a right or wrong answer, in fact it is still open-ended because as we discussed in Chapter 2, the children are honest in their responses. Very often they will reply to a question like this with responses like "Not really," or "I don't know."

Sometimes Caryn and Patty ask more direct questions to establish that a certain result does or does not occur, as in the following example about an activity in which the children make sugar crystals:

CARYN: Did the sugar dissolve?

KRISSY: No.

CARYN: What do you think is a reason why the sugar might not have dissolved?

KRISSY: Too much sugar.

CARYN: Too much sugar. Well . . .

KRISSY: *(Interrupts)* Way too much.

Caryn does not necessarily know how Krissy will answer her question. Either a positive or negative response could be followed by an interchange that might help Krissy to think about reasons why the sugar did or did not dissolve. Note that when Krissy tells Caryn that the sugar didn't dissolve, Caryn does not evaluate her response, but rather asks another question. In this kind of exchange, Caryn narrows the focus to one particular aspect of the activity and then asks the children to think of an explanation. It's interesting here to note that their observation is correct in a sense, but that the group actually had added too little water, having measured incorrectly. The sugar was excessive only in proportion to the amount of water that they used. Their analysis is still accurate however, and Caryn is able to build upon their observation.

Both through such direct questions or through questions that follow a child's line of reasoning to jointly establish a result, Patty and Caryn often help students to focus on one part of an extremely varied experience, a part that can then become the object of explicit thought.

Types of Second-Grade Science Talk

One problem that we face in thinking about science talk in the second grade is that on the surface these young children do not sound very "scientific," if we employ the characteristics usually associated with the language of science as used by adults. The scientific register, such as that found in textbooks and journals, is described by Lemke (1990) as serious and dignified in tone, verbally explicit, containing technical terms and causal language, while avoiding colloquialisms, figurative language, personal reference, and narrative. Obviously children do not sound like science textbooks when they discuss their activities. Yet we believe that there are parallels between the children's wrap-up discussions and what is done, said, and written in the adult scientific community. It follows from that belief that they are learning how to "talk science."

According to *Benchmarks for Science Literacy,* a central question throughout the grades should be: "How do we know that's true?" (4). This question is raised and explored in second-grade science talks through what we call "reasoning episodes." These are sequences in which a child makes a statement, Patty or Caryn then asks her to justify that statement and then the child offers an explanation or a prediction. In these reasoning episodes, Caryn and Patty are supporting children to make claims about science activities and to justify those claims. This can be seen as the very beginning of the coordination of theories and evidence that is central both to scientific discourse (Kuhn 1993) and to thinking and talking in school more generally.

Our first detailed examination of these episodes was done from a research perspective, when Maureen was working on her dissertation (Reddy 1994). She used the qualitative approach of inductive analysis (Erickson 1986) and identified three categories of talk used by children in reasoning episodes. The three categories emerged from analysis of wrap-up transcripts representing the 1992–1993 school year, the first year that we worked together, but we have repeatedly found that they apply equally well to the wrap-ups that took place in subsequent years. These are the three categories:

1. what we call "observation," when children provide sensory information about the activity that they are reporting on

2. what we refer to as "tool," when they provide information that goes beyond their own senses to some tool that the culture provides to augment sensory information, like counting or measuring

3. what we have termed "theory," when children offer explanations, hypotheses, or predictions

After identifying these three categories in wrap-up, we read the book *Science for All Americans* (1990), a publication of the American Association for the Advancement of Science about scientific literacy. This book has also been very helpful to us in our thinking about habits of mind. In a chapter entitled "The Nature of Science," the authors, Rutherford and Ahlgren, outline three strategies that parallel our three categories. They begin by describing the scientific process:

> Scientific inquiry is not easily described apart from the context of particular investigations. There simply is no fixed set of steps that scientists always follow, no one path that leads them unerringly to scientific knowledge. There are, however, certain features of science that give it a distinctive character as a mode of inquiry. Although those features are especially characteristic of the work of professional scientists, everyone can exercise them in thinking scientifically about many matters of interest in everyday life.

Next, they talk about observation:

> Sooner or later, the validity of scientific claims is settled by referring to observations of phenomena.

They then refer to tools:

> To make their observations, scientists use their own senses, instruments (such as microscopes) that enhance those senses, and instruments that tap characteristics quite different from what humans can sense (such as magnetic fields).

And last, they mention theories:

> Scientists strive to make sense of observations of phenomena by inventing explanations for them that use, or are consistent with, currently accepted scientific principles. Such explanations—theories—may be either sweeping or restricted, but they must be logically sound and incorporate a significant body of scientifically valid observations. (5–7)

As this passage shows, the three categories, observation, tool, and theory, which emerged from analysis of Patty and Caryn's wrap-up discussions with second graders, are analogous to ways of thinking that are accepted in the scientific community.

Certainly, we do not want to overstate this claim, and readily acknowledge that there are vast differences between the children's uses of observation, tool, and theory and how adult scientists use these processes. Nonetheless, we feel that it is valid to claim that children are learning to "talk science," because in reasoning episodes, Caryn and Patty are supporting children to justify and predict in ways that are widely valued in the scientific community. Having said this, we want to give fuller descriptions and examples of the three categories.

Observation

Not surprisingly, children frequently demonstrate that they observed what happened in their activities as they talk about what they experienced. Observations are defined as statements that provide sensory information about the activity that children are reporting about. They may be descriptions of how something looked, sounded, smelled, felt, or tasted. Observations also include phenomena that children experienced through their senses, such as saying that something fell, or overflowed. In addition, this category includes simple perceptual comparisons, such as those using the words "more" or "less."

In many cases, children spontaneously offer "what happened" observations at the beginning of their reports, even before the teachers ask any questions. For example, in a report about an activity in which children learned how to use litmus paper, Colleen, the reporter, begins this way:

COLLEEN: Well today we had a little accident. The ammonia spilt all over and it smelled. And these are what we tried (*Holds up a paper towel with bits of litmus paper stuck to it*) . . . Some of the litmus paper.

CARYN: Um hm.

COLLEEN: And this one was tea and it turned . . . it turned blue. And this one was soapy water and that one just stayed purple and this one was lemon juice and it stayed purple too. And this one was . . . ammonia and it . . . and this one was kinda purple and this one was a solution of dry milk and this one turned different colors.

Here, Colleen starts with a mishap, but goes on to give a great deal of observational information, telling how the litmus paper looked as a result of their testing with various liquids. This is her independent beginning which is basically a long initial turn. Caryn's only contribution is "um hm," which is technically called a "backchannel," a signal to a conversational partner that you are listening. As this and many other examples show, children successfully use observation as a way to tell what happened in their activities. Such observations tell the rest of the class what the group experienced.

Children not only offer observations spontaneously in their reports, they also receive teacher support to justify their claims in reasoning episodes by using their own observations. These episodes exemplify the beginning of a scientific use of observation, since sensory information is being marshaled as evidence to justify claims or to support theories. That is, the teacher's thinking questions help the children to select something that is "worth observing" (Millar and Driver 1987) from among all the things that happened, and to use it as a way to justify or predict.

The following is a simple and straightforward example of observation used for justification from a report about an activity in which children had to use their senses to identify various unlabeled substances:

PATTY: You liked the flour the best! OK . . . Why did you think, John, the flour was the flour? . . . John, why did you think the flour was the flour?

JOHN: Because it tasted like it.

Here, John was asked to justify his opinion that one of the unidentified powders that the group was given was flour. He does so by noting an observation based on taste.

Another example comes from a report about a balance activity:

PATTY: Oh so did you try to make it balance? In this game?

ASHA: No not really it just balanced by itself.

PATTY: How could you tell if it was balanced?

ASHA: Cause you could see if it slanted down.

PATTY: Oh I see. Did everyone hear that or should she repeat that? How Asha could tell if it was balanced . . . Could you say that again?

ASHA: You could see if it slanted down.

Patty's first question helps Asha to establish that the scale balanced. Patty asks Asha how she could tell that the scale was balanced, and Asha justifies her statement with an observation.

Tool

When providing justifications that are classified as "tool" responses, children refer to some tool that the culture provides to amplify their sensory information. We use the word "tool" in the way that Vygotsky uses it: a culturally developed means for supporting thinking (Wertsch 1991). Tools may either be concrete, such as the actual balance scale that the children use in an activity, or psychological, such as counting. As cognitive scientist Lauren Resnick points out:

> Almost all real-world mental activity involves the use of tools that expand people's mental power. These tools can be as complex as computer simulation programs or as simple as lists of frequently used calculations, but they are almost always present. (1989, 12)

In wrap-up, tools help reporters by giving them ways to justify their results or opinions that go beyond their own observations. Examples of tools used in wrap-up are counting, measuring, and referring to recording sheets, task cards, charts, or other print in the environment. Tools can provide tangible support for the job of reporting, for example when Curtis brought a task card up and used its steps to sequence his report. Children also justify with tools when they use an object to demonstrate, for example, Rodney, who used the balance arm. Like those based on observations, tool justifications are concrete in that they are rooted in the actual experience of the activity, or physical props.

As with the category of observation, children spontaneously refer to tools when they begin reports and also use them in reasoning episodes. In the following example, Emma, the reporter, tells about an activity in which her group has built a structure from straws, and has predicted how many cuts they could make before it fell. They then actually cut it to see how well they had predicted:

EMMA: We had no fights and we had to use twenty straws to build a structure and we cut it fifty times and we didn't get to finish.

CARYN: Fifty times and it didn't collapse yet?

EMMA: *(Nods)*

Emma uses counting to describe what happened in the activity. She may well have exaggerated the number of cuts that her group made in an effort to impress her audience. Oftentimes children seem to use tools to give external authority to what they are saying, a phenomenon that also exists in the scientific community (Latour and Woolgar 1986; Lemke

1990). Children appear to know that an argument may be more sensible or stronger when buttressed by evidence of having counted or measured something, for example, when George claimed, "You *hafta* count how many things you have when you balance."

As with observations, Caryn and Patty support children to use tools to justify or predict. The following is a tool example from a reasoning episode about the same straw structure activity in Patty's room, in a wrap-up conducted by Heidi Miller, a student teacher from Clark University:

HEIDI: Do you think it would stay if you cut it there?

TARA: *(Shakes head)*

HEIDI: No? Why not?

TARA: Because it would fall.

HEIDI: Do you know why it would fall? Why do you think it would fall?

TARA: Cuz there's only three things. *(Points)*

HEIDI: Cuz there's only three things if you cut it there? Oh I see. So what would that cause it to be then? Would that be balanced?

TARA: *(Shakes head)* It'd be crooked.

After Tara predicts that the structure would fall if one leg were cut, Heidi asks her to reason about why that would happen. Her answer, "Cuz there's only three things," shows that she is counting an uneven number of remaining supports. Furthermore, her use of the word "only" suggests that she thinks that three is an insufficient number.

Another type of tool commonly used by children is environmental print, one that is readily accessible because Caryn and Patty have many signs and charts hanging in their rooms. In the following example, George is explaining an activity in which his group made shapes with rubber bands on a geo board and then measured their perimeter. Many children, including George, have trouble pronouncing perimeter; many others got so carried away with making the shapes that they never measured them, and so have little idea about what perimeter is. Patty has just asked what the name of the activity is, trying to call their attention to the fact that the title of the task is a key to what they were supposed to have done:

GEORGE: Permitter shapes.

PATTY: Perimeter shapes. What does that mean, perimeter shapes? . . . What does that mean? . . . Here Steven. Call on someone and see what they have to say . . . Do you know what it means, perimeter shapes?

GEORGE: Total length of all . . . sides of an object.

PATTY: Ah! Say that one more time.

GEORGE: The total length of all sides of an object.

George's very succinct and correct definition comes from a vocabulary chart hanging on the wall nearby. Patty goes on to congratulate him for having the idea to consult the chart and read the definition from it as a way to suggest to the audience that they, too, can productively use the information that is in the room.

Theory

The definition of a scientific theory is usually quite stringent, involving at minimum a causal mechanism and having general applicability across cases (Chinn and Brewer 1993). However, the seven-year-olds in Patty's and Caryn's classes use what Kuhn, Amsel, and O'Laughlin (1988) call the "simplest, most fundamental theory in scientific thinking: a theory asserting a relationship between one category of phenomena and another" (8). Some of their theories are explanations, dealing with relationships such as cause and effect, sometimes marked by the use of because or "cuz." Often, children explain why they performed their activity in a certain way. In doing so, they reveal their working theory, or what has been called a "theory in action" (Karmiloff-Smith and Inhelder 1975). Theories can also be used to predict what might occur in the future, though they are usually not expressed as scientific hypotheses that are testable.

When we began to analyze transcripts, we could find many theories, at almost an intuitive level, but we needed a good working definition that would allow us to categorize and reliably identify them. A quote from Gordon Wells helped us to come up with some characteristics of the theories that we found. According to Wells (1992), stating a theory "demonstrates how one can extrapolate from a range of specific experiences a principle which applies to those past experiences and possibly to some similar future ones as well" (8). Now we realize that when children provide theory responses, they often construct generalizations that go beyond their experiments, expressing principles that apply not only to their specific activity. This generalization is expressed in the way that they talk. Their theories often contain present-tense verbs, use of general pronouns (you versus we), indefinite versus definite articles, modal verbs (for example, would), and terms that are not just observations (for example, dissolve instead of disappear).

The following is a theory example from Caryn's room. Sam is describing the popcorn activity:

CARYN: Sam you want to say something. I know I want to hear it. You told me in the group. What does the foil do when you put the foil over the top of the popcorn?

SAM: Keeps the heat in.

CARYN: Keeps the heat in. Do you think that it makes . . . what does that make the popcorn do?

SAM: Pop.

CARYN: Pop what? Do you think it would make it pop faster or pop slower?

SAM: Faster.

CARYN: Faster . . . and why?

SAM: *(Looks at the ceiling)* Well if . . . if you didn't have um foil over it the heat would be coming out.

CARYN: Uh huh!

This whole excerpt is one reasoning episode in which there are several turns by Sam that express his theory about the importance of having the foil covering the test tube. First, he says that the foil "keeps the heat in." Then he predicts that the foil would make the popcorn pop faster. Last, he gives an explanation why: "If you didn't have foil over it the heat would be coming out." In each case, he makes a generalization that goes beyond his particular activity. He uses the present-tense "keeps the heat in", and the generalized "you" instead of first-person pronouns. Here, Caryn is helping Sam to make his thinking public. She herself already knows what he thinks because he told her privately in the group; she wants him to articulate his theory to the whole group so that other children can reflect and build on it.

Theory Co-construction

It is important to note that Sam's theory is supported by the questions that Caryn asks and, more precisely, the way in which she asks them. This is a process that we call theory co-construction because the children's theories emerge during the conversation with the teachers. They are not presented by the children on their own, but rather, through the questions and answers of the dialogue itself, a theory emerges across the turns of both speakers. As we said and showed above, children frequently use both observation and tool on their own as ways to spontaneously start their reports. However, we have found that they very rarely provide theories without teacher support. In fact, for the 1992–1993 school year in both classrooms, we counted and discovered that spontaneous theories only happened twice, and then at only the very end of the year. For all the years that we have been studying wrap-up, we have found that almost all theories are co-constructed in dialogue with teachers during wrap-up discussions.

This fact means that there is a contrast between observation and tool on the one hand, and theory on the other. For observation and tool, the teachers' support consists of providing a new function for forms that the children spontaneously offer. In other words, on their own in relating "what happened" reporters often tell what things look like, or count how many objects they have. But, they seldom use observations or counting on their own to support their statements or to explain or justify. There-fore, Patty and Caryn are helping children to expand the ways in which they talk about observation and tool by using them to reason about the activities, not just to describe them. In contrast, the children with whom we work seldom spontaneously offer theories. Caryn and Patty provide a different type of support for children's theories in reasoning episodes by helping children to construct theories in the dialogue. This is what we mean by co-construction, as we will show in the examples that follow.

Although children often use "because" or "cuz" when telling what happened or to discuss interpersonal disputes, when they respond to the teachers' questions in reasoning episodes they usually do not use causal language. Rather, students give simple answers that would not be clas-sified as explanations or theories if their turn were taken out of context. For example, consider this example about the popcorn activity:

MORRIS: Um we . . . we let the test tube go around and first . . . the first time we were doing the popcorn it burnt so we had to . . . we had to do it over again.

CARYN: Why do you think it might have burned?

MORRIS: There was too much oil in it.

CARYN: Too much oil? What about the second time? What made it right?

MORRIS: Um . . . um there was less oil in it.

Here, Morris states his theory in response to Caryn's question asking why he thought the popcorn burnt. His response is a simple declarative sentence: "There was too much oil in it." We can infer that this sentence is his explanation because he answers a question that asks for an explanation.

The same phenomenon occurs with children's one-word utterances when combined with teachers' questions. In this example from the same report, Caryn asks about the change of the kernel:

CARYN: What kind of change did the popcorn go through?

MORRIS: First it was regular, then it burnt, then it popped.

CARYN: Then it popped. And what made that change?

MORRIS: Um the fire.

Morris states the theory that the fire caused the popcorn to pop. He does this by giving a one-word response which, when combined with Caryn's question, becomes his explanation.

It is important to emphasize here, however, that co-construction of theories does not represent a one-way cause and effect in which a teacher's question creates a child's theory. To illustrate what we mean, we will use another excerpt from a popcorn report. Rick, the reporter, has said that this group varied the amount of oil in the test tube:

CARYN: So what would happen if you didn't put any oil over it?

RICK: It popped. It made a noise. It jumped up a little.

Here, Caryn's question would seem to be a theoretical one that asks for a prediction, but then Rick gives an observation. In other words, we do not consider a child's response to be a theory simply because it follows a teacher's question that would support a justification or a hypothesis.

Some Guidelines for Supporting Science Talk

Patty and Caryn must use a wide variety of discourse strategies in their effort to provide support for children in wrap-up. We have come to see that the teacher's role is to scaffold the children's talk. The strongest version of teacher support is the kind of co-construction discussed above, where theories are actually created in the dialogue itself.

The purpose of scaffolding, as the metaphor suggests, is to create a temporary structure that, over time, is owned by the child. Therefore, Caryn and Patty find ways to help the children talk about science which are just ahead of what the children seem to be able to do on their own, using Vygotsky's theory of the Zone of Proximal Development, "the distance between the actual developmental level as determined by independent problem solving and the level of potential development as determined through problem solving under adult guidance or in collaboration with more capable peers" (Vygotsky 1978, 86).

This kind of teaching and talking is highly individualized because the teacher always has to respond to whatever a child says and proceed jointly from that beginning. The teachers have to be prepared for, and accepting of, almost anything.

Helping Every Child to Be the Reporter

The challenge for Patty and Caryn is to build on what children say and to elicit information about the science content. What about the most challenging situation, the silent child? Remember that the role of reporter rotates so that very shy and reticent children take their turn along with those who happily volunteer to speak whenever they can. The role of reporter is an important opportunity for every child to have the chance for extended dialogue with the teacher and his or her peers, but we also know that some children, especially at the beginning of the year, can find the role burdensome and frightening. Caryn has already related the story about Tina, who complained of "chest pains" due to the stress!

From the beginning of the year, Caryn and Patty insist that everyone must play his or her role, yet they take seriously some children's difficulty in giving reports. To deal with this predicament, they have come up with many ways to offer support and encouragement. Reporters come to sit or stand next to the teacher, who sits at their level. Caryn allows them to sit in her "big blue chair" in the front; Patty often assembles a panel of reporters who sit together for support while she takes a seat in the back with the rest of the class. Sometimes reporters will bring up their whole group for moral support as long as the other children are not allowed to take over the report. For those who have trouble starting, Patty and Caryn suggest entry points into a report which rely on external support. For instance, children can always begin with the name of their activity, and many say "We did . . . ," filling in the blank with the title, for example, "We did the Bridge of Strength." Another nonthreatening way to begin is to list the materials as in the following example from the beginning of the year in Patty's class. The reporter is Manuel, a child whom you met in Chapter 3 when we showed an example in which his group decided to use the base that he built for their joint straw structure:

PATTY: Go ahead Manuel tell the group what you did.

(Manuel does not respond.)

PATTY: What materials did you use?

MANUEL: Lemon.

PATTY: Lemon.

MANUEL: Water . . . tea . . . soapy water . . . milk.

PATTY: That's right. This is the group that used what kind of paper did you use?

(Manuel does not respond.)

PATTY: What kind of paper? *(Long pause)* You know Manuel came and asked me for that word before. Litmus paper. So you say you used litmus paper. When you put the paper in what colors did it change?

MANUEL: Purple blue.

Notice how much help Manuel gets with his report. Patty knows that he has heard about litmus paper because, as she says, he questioned her about it during the activity. She asks him for the name and waits for his response, and then supplies it for him, bringing it into the conversation as though he had responded: "So you say you used litmus paper."

Another example from later in the year shows how another reporter uses this same strategy to help herself when she has trouble at the beginning. She is presenting an activity in which her group added vinegar to various substances to watch for chemical reactions:

PATTY: Go ahead Asha.

ASHA: We did the um *(Shrugs shoulders, long pause).*

PATTY: Do you need help from someone in your group?

(Asha shakes her head no.)

PATTY: No? Do you want to try it by yourself? OK let me ask you a question.

ASHA: I can.

PATTY: OK go ahead.

ASHA: We used vinegar, sugar, baking soda, and flour.

PATTY: OK and what did you do with them?

ASHA: We poured the vinegar on . . . on 'em and we'd see *(Spoken quietly while facing Patty, back to the other kids)*. We poured the vinegar.

PATTY: OK tell the group. You did what? Here tell the group. You're doing a wonderful job Asha but you have to tell the group. Go ahead . . . You said it perfectly.

ASHA: We had to pour a little vinegar and see what happened . . . if it changed or not . . . like bubbling up or fizzing.

Asha has appropriated the strategy of using a list of materials as a way to begin her report, after having some difficulty beginning. It is particularly striking that when Patty suggests that she might need help from a group member, she rejects the offer and says "I can." What she can indeed do is begin by listing the materials. Thus, a strategy that was offered by Patty in the past became one that Asha is able to use independently. After Asha lists the materials, she can answer Patty's question about what the group did and even state the purpose of the experiment. This example shows the child as learner taking ownership over more of the task, by using a strategy that formerly belonged to the teacher. It shows the teacher's scaffold that was used with Manuel acted as a temporary structure, later owned by the children.

Another way that Caryn has helped reticent reporters like Tina is by suggesting that the audience ask questions first. When a child comes up and silently stands there, she asks, "Would you like the group to ask you some questions?" This means that the reporter does not have to think about how to begin and break the silence by taking the first turn. All he or she has to do is answer what is asked. For many children it is easier to respond than to generate the first turn, and after a couple of questions, they get up their confidence to continue.

As Asha did with listing materials, Ramone took up this strategy on his own in March when he had trouble thinking of what to say. He went to the reporter's chair in the middle of the circle of his classmates, but sat there unable to begin:

RAMONE: Would it be okay if they ask like three questions because I have to think, cuz I forgot a couple things.

CARYN: Okay, raise your hand if you have a question or comment.

Building on What the Children Say

In talking about strategies to help children who are shy or reluctant—such as listing materials—we want to emphasize that such beginnings are accepted just as positively as a turn that describes the activity in detail. It is absolutely imperative that Caryn and Patty accept each report if the rotating role is going to work. Children are encouraged to do the best job of reporter that they can, based upon their own ability to construct a recount and upon what their group accomplished.

Both Patty and Caryn discourage children from writing and then reading their reports. We have found that a written report creates many problems because children often have trouble reading their own and each other's writing and spelling. Sometimes another child in the group writes the whole report and the reporter has no ownership of the information.

More importantly, though, we also feel that as much as possible wrap-up should be a conversation in which children are encouraged to use what Barnes (1992) refers to as "exploratory talk" (28). In the following example, Luke is presenting the activity in which his group has cooked a raisin in a test tube and in the process they have created what they call "juice":

LUKE: Well after you know we put the test tube over the uh candle we put water in it and it started . . . you know like when you make like tea and it starts bubbling so much? It did that. And then after we did it we dumped it into this cup and there was all this like juice in there and we grabbed it and we got it in here [the paper cup] but it all it got all sticky now it's all sticky right on here.

CARYN: So you're saying . . . do you think that the juice leaked out because you added more water? Did you have juice leaking out before? Because there was clearly juice on the side of this test tube. It was brown. It wasn't just water.

LUKE: It probably just took up . . . you know like the outside, how it probably just . . . how it . . . you know the raisin's brown and it took half of the top off instead of . . . this might not even be the juice . . . instead of juice the water you know like it took the color out . . . the color off?

CARYN: Oh. So his explanation might be that instead of it being the juice it took the color of the burnt stuff on the side of the test tube? Is that what you said?

LUKE: Yeah . . . of the raisin.

CARYN: On the raisin.

ANDY: It's like food coloring.

CARYN: Oh like a dye.

It's easy to see in this example that Luke is thinking on-line. Although the members of his group got together to discuss the content of their report, he obviously has not rehearsed the form in which he presents their information, as you can tell by his hesitations and repetitions. Also, his language demonstrates that he is considering possibilities: He says "probably" twice and also uses "might." In addition, his second turn ends with a rising intonation which suggests that he is asking as much as he is telling.

Another interesting and important aspect of this exchange is that Caryn is getting new insights also. The word "so" is what is called a discourse marker (Schiffrin 1987), indicating that Caryn is trying to make an inference based on what Luke said. Then she hesitates and asks additional clarifying questions. Although Luke agrees with her that the water got its color from the "burnt stuff on the side of the test tube" he actually says that the color came from the raisin itself, which she repeats. It's an analogy offered by Andy, another member of the group (when he says "It's like food coloring") that helps her to see what they're talking about. The discourse marker "Oh" occurs twice and suggests that she was orienting to new information. This example shows that interpreting children's responses is often not easy, but it is imperative for the teachers to understand what the children mean if they are to build on what they say.

This kind of teacher insight is one aspect of wrap-up that contributes to its conversational feel even though it is a school-based and teacher-moderated speech event. Caryn and Patty often ask the children for clarification if they truly don't understand something. In addition, they ask fewer questions to which they already know the answer than is typical in traditional classroom discourse. This makes a big difference in the quality of talk because the children know that the teachers are truly interested in what they have to say. This means, of course, that Patty and Caryn cannot usually ask prepared questions since topics arise naturally as they would in conversation. Of course, there are questions that are kept alive throughout a unit, often those that relate to the "big idea." For instance, Caryn's question about the foil on the test tube is one that recurs for almost every group. However, when a question is repeated to several reporters, it is done in the spirit of gathering different theories, not as a fishing expedition to replace one response with a "better" one. The next example illustrates how children's own theories are valued. Again, these excerpts come from the popcorn experiment:

CARYN: OK my big question to you and I asked you this . . . I wonder if you can answer me. Ready? Rodney found out . . . his group found out that it took longer . . . longer to pop the popcorn without the tinfoil and it took a shorter time you told me with the tinfoil on.

CHILD: I know why.

CARYN: Do you have an explanation for that?

RODNEY: Umm *(Long pause)* maybe because the heatness and the coolness on the . . . without the tinfoil it's cooling the . . . the breeze was pushing the thing over . . . the fire. Blowing it over and it keeps coming out.

CARYN: Out of the test tube you mean?

RODNEY: No. Like the wind would still be . . . pushing the fire over on the side.

CARYN: Oh so you think that it didn't matter if the tinfoil was on or off?

RODNEY: Yeah.

CARYN: It was the wind coming through the window blowing the flame?

RODNEY: Yeah.

Caryn poses her frequent question about the tinfoil. From experience, she knows that children can often explain this phenomenon. She of course knows the answer to this question. Rodney states his theory that the breeze was pushing the fire, and says, "It keeps coming out." Caryn asks an honest clarifying question, "Out of the test tube you mean?" and gets a direct answer, "No," plus a clarification. Rodney thinks that the wind from the open window blew the flame over. He probably means "It [the fire] keeps *going* out," rather than "coming out." His explanation is not what Caryn expects, which is that the tinfoil traps the heat inside. As in the example above, her use of the discourse marker "Oh" indicates that she has a new insight. She does not correct him, though, and the conversation continues:

CARYN: OK. A couple of people have their hands raised. I don't know if you want to call on them.

RODNEY: Mark?

MARK: I know why it does that. Because when you put the tinfoil on . . . when you put it in there's more heat . . . because when you put it on . . . because it's blocking . . . when it goes up, the heat . . . can't get out so it gets hotter in there so it pops faster.

CARYN: OK that . . . that was something different from what Rodney said. Do you understand what Mark just said?

RODNEY: Yeah.

CARYN: He thought that because the tinfoil was on top the heat couldn't get out. What do you think about that? *(Long pause)* Do you think it would have been hotter or cooler in the test tube without the tinfoil?

RODNEY: Cooler.

CARYN: Cooler. And it did take longer didn't it . . . to cook without the tinfoil? Do you think that has something . . .

RODNEY: *(Interrupts)* Two minutes and fifty-eight seconds I think.

CARYN: And two minutes and four seconds with it . . . with it on. So do you think that that could be an explanation? *(Long pause)* The tinfoil kept the heat inside the test tube . . . it was hotter?

RODNEY: Yyyyeah *(Very hesitant)*.

CARYN: Could be.

Mark offers an opposing theory (which happens to be the correct one that Caryn was looking for). Instead of saying that one child is right and the other one is wrong, she very deliberately juxtaposes these two theories, restating Mark's view and building upon it with questions that pertain to evidence supporting that theory. Note that even at the end Caryn leaves acceptance of this theory up to Rodney, the reporter, whose tone suggests that he may not agree. This exchange exemplifies an important quality of wrap-up, that the teachers are more interested in engaging children in thinking about the activities than in producing correct responses in which the children themselves do not believe.

The American Association for the Advancement of Science describes a similar practice as one of its *Benchmarks for Science Literacy* for grades three through five: "As explanations take on more and more importance, teachers must insist that students pay attention to the explanations of others and remain open to new ideas. This is an appropriate time to introduce the idea that in science it is legitimate to offer different explanations of the same set of observations, although this notion is apparently difficult for many youngsters to comprehend" (1993, 11).

As a way to characterize wrap-up, we return to "instructional conversations" as described by Goldenberg (1992/1993) who claims that such conversations have two major dimensions, each of which is associated with several elements. Instructional attributes are the following: thematic focus, activation and use of background and relevant schemata, direct teaching, promotion of more complex language, and expression and elicitation of bases for statements and positions. Conversational attributes include: fewer "known answer" questions, responsivity to student contributions, connected discourse, a challenging but nonthreatening atmosphere and general participation (319).

In order for these rich instructional conversations to qualify as science talk, teachers must keep the science content as the main topic. As you have seen throughout this book, talking about science content is never a given because the social aspects of groupwork are a continual concern for children and their teachers. As often as possible, Caryn and Patty nudge the reporter back to the scientific topic of the activity that the group has done. When children are talking about science, teachers then can guide them to select a more narrow focus, helping them to pay attention to important attributes of their experiments. Most important, though, is giving children practice at answering the question "How do you know?" by engaging in reasoning episodes with them.

5 *Dialogue Journals in Science*

Please no more challenges.

—Andy, a second grader

As most of us realize through repeated interactions with those around us, words and actions sometimes conflict. Such is the case with Andy, quoted above, who wrote "Please no more challenges," but came bouncing up to Caryn's desk to await her response to his journal entry. Andy, like most of Caryn's second graders, exudes an excitement about and investment in his dialogue journal work. We attribute his enthusiasm in part to the fact that Caryn's journals are more immediate than traditional dialogue journals. Typically such journals are used in classrooms where children write in response to the literature that they read (Atwell 1987) or about self-chosen topics (Staton, Shuy, Peyton, and Reed 1988). A teacher takes them, responds, and returns them for children to read at a later time. In this chapter we will show how dialogue journals, conceptualized as "written conversations" (Short, Harste, and Burke 1996), can be an important tool for science teaching and learning.

Caryn's Story

Sitting at my desk after science, during journal writing, was the only part of the day I considered peaceful. For my second graders it was a time to quietly engage in science writing. For me it was a time to catch up on the daily teacher tasks of writing notes to parents, correcting, and record keeping. About three minutes after he began writing, Kyle yelled, "Miss McCrohon, I'm done." He had just finished the sixth activity from a Balance and Structure unit with Nancy, Miguel, and Emma. It involved having the children balance on a life-sized seesaw that was brought into the classroom. Kyle was a bright-eyed, energetic, curious second grader

89

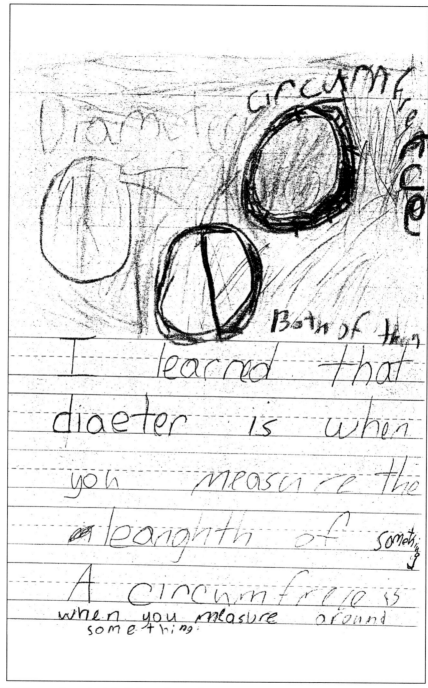

5–1 A page from Andy's dialogue journal

Could you give a better
explanation of diameter?

Diameter is when

you measure in

the middle of

somthing.
In the middle of what? a lake
a bananna a what?

of a shape.

of course!
what kind of shape?

like

a flat circle.

(Continued)

who was always willing to finish his work quickly, so that he could do a free time activity. Wondering to myself about how Kyle could be finished so soon I said, "Oh really, let me read it." He came to my desk and read: "I did balance with Nancy. I found out I weighed a lot."

After he finished reading this to me, I told him that his entry didn't tell me what he learned about the activity. My goal was for him to write about the relationship between weight, distance, and balance. I knew that he was beginning to understand this relationship because of the explanation he had offered during our wrap-up discussion. I began rattling off questions to him and asked him to go back and try again. He was angry. As he walked back to his seat, I heard him mumbling to himself "How am I going to remember all those questions?" I hate to admit it now, but at first I felt like telling him to keep his comments to himself and get to work. Luckily, I didn't. I realized that his complaint was reasonable. How was this seven-year-old going to remember the four or five questions I quickly asked him before I sent him on his way? I went over to his seat and read his entry over again and based on what he had written, I wrote down the following question, "Did you and Nancy weigh the same?" I then went back to my tasks, to give him time to write. He answered my question and brought it up for me to read. His response was, "We didn't balance at all." I wrote another question based on his response. We went back and forth five more times:

Did Emma and Miguel get the seesaw to balance?

Yes.

Do they weigh the same?

No.

How did they get the seesaw to balance?

Miguel moved to the fulcrum.

Why does that make a difference?

When you move to the fulcrum you weigh less.

Why?

Because the distance.

By the end of my exchanges with Kyle I was satisfied and he had a great sense of accomplishment. It was obvious to me that Kyle understood the difficult questions that I asked him. I started dialoguing with my students the very next day. This is how my dialogue journals began. It was a fluke. It just happened.

Well, the thirty minutes of peace that I usually had when my kids wrote in their science journals was gone. I now had kids lined up three and four at a time waiting to be "challenged." (We called my questions challenge questions.) Questions had to be personal and tailored to each child's particular journal entry. I could not use a prescribed set of questions from a teacher's manual because I wanted to use the child's entry as a starting point. My goal was to bring the children to a higher level of understanding, thinking, and writing, so I always tried to pose questions that would encourage the children to think more deeply about the activities. I had to be a quick thinker and write quickly because of the many eager writers that awaited me.

My hope was for them to get their thoughts and ideas down on paper. I had a lot of kids in my classroom, like Kyle, who didn't know how to get beyond a one-line entry. I wanted to change that. From questioning them orally, I knew that many of my students understood more than they were writing in their journals. What impressed me the most during our group discussions was hearing the kids making real-world connections, hypothesizing, problem solving, defining, and theorizing. Dialoguing enabled me to draw out this information in their writing.

Throughout the rest of the year we wrote together and the kids enjoyed this immensely. They would come up to me as quickly as possible with big smiles on their faces, ready for their challenge. Some, after four or five exchanges with me, would roll their eyes and stamp their feet. I could tell from their expressions that they were wondering, "What else could she possibly ask?" As I watched them go back to their seats, though, they would be all smiles, bragging to neighbors along the way that this was their fifth challenge of the day. I knew then that I had found a solution to a problem that began more than a year before. Watching them go back to their seats, I thought of Kyle and the first time we dialogued together. I realize now that this was not just a "fluke." There were many events involved in the evolution of dialogue journals.

Was It a Fluke?

The beginning seeds for dialogue journals were planted during my first year of teaching. As you know, my assignment was to teach second grade in a new inner-city school that put special emphasis on science and technology. You also are already aware that the school had adopted for its science program a cooperative, hands-on, discovery approach called Complex Instruction

In September of 1992 I was set to start implementing my science program. I began by teaching my students skillbuilding games that would help them learn how to work cooperatively in groups. In October we started our first science curriculum unit. Everything seemed to be going very smoothly. I was happy to see my students working together and being on task. During wrap-up discussions the reporters were not as hesitant to speak in front of their audience as I feared they might be. I was trying to pose "how" and "why" questions that would help my students hypothesize, explain, and elaborate, and they were succeeding. I was a happy teacher! Then I started to assess the worksheets that went along with the curriculum. What I received were blank worksheets, or partially completed worksheets that did not really show me if the child had actually grasped the important aspects of the activities. I was disappointed because after listening to their highly engaging talk during whole-class discussion, I felt that their worksheets did not represent their knowledge. This was the only kind of individual accountability that I had.

Well, needless to say I had a little chat with my students about the importance of filling out their worksheets. I told them that this was a way for me to find out what they were learning. We continued the science activities with the children promising to fill out the whole worksheet.

For the most part the worksheets were coming in filled out, but I quickly discovered that they did not help me assess what the children were learning. The worksheets required the children to record results, or answer one or two factual questions. They did not ask the type of questions that stimulated descriptions of procedures, explanations, or even children's general thinking about the activities.

I went to my principal, Dr. Joan Merrill, with my concerns about the worksheets. Together we discussed solutions to this problem. We decided that each child should keep a science journal. We thought that by reading their journal entries I would be better able to assess what the children were gleaning from the activities. So starting in December, until the end of the school year, my students kept science journals.

Once we were finished with our wrap-up my students had about thirty minutes to write a journal entry and draw a picture to go with the entry. At first I was a bit weary. Science was taking longer than expected, out of our seven-hour day. My principal said not to worry because science journals are part of language arts and she was excited to see writing across the curriculum.

In journal writing there were no set rules. The children used inventive spelling. I did not object if periods or capitals were missing. I wanted them to be free to write without worrying about spelling and grammar rules. The range of writing about their work varied greatly, due to the fact the each child could freely choose what he or she wanted to write about.

As the months went by I began to notice a pattern throughout most of the journals. The majority of entries were about the process that occurred during the activity. Even immediately following productive wrap-up discussions the children were not putting more than their procedural knowledge down on paper. I knew that I could not individually question every student during wrap-up, but even the reporters who were answering my questions orally were not writing their knowledge down in their journals. I ended my first year of teaching knowing that the science journals were not meeting my expectations.

In September of 1993, I thought I would introduce the journals in a different way, telling my new students that I already knew what they did during science, and that now I wanted them to write about what they learned. Well guess what I got again? The dreaded one- or two-line entries that told what they *did* during science, not what they *learned.*

Two months later, in November, we began a new unit on structure and balance. Kyle was calling. His voice called us to a new beginning—dialogue journals. I was no longer an evaluator but a *collaborator.* I have found that on the second-grade level in order for children to produce significant scientific writing, it is important to have direct teacher support.

Using Dialogue Journals in the Classroom

Children usually begin by writing a narrative that tells about the process of doing their activity. Many are procedural recounts similar to their oral reports. For ease of reading the following examples, we have standardized spelling and punctuation. The child's turns are in standard print, whereas Caryn's turns are in italics.

In this first example, after completing the experiment in which his group added sugar to boiling water to create a solution that over time will form sugar crystals, Rodney writes:

> In my group we had to take some water and put it in a pan. And then we put sugar in it too. And then we took a stick and string and tied it on the stick and put washers on the end.

Rodney's entry is essentially a recount of what his group accomplished. Although he uses first-person pronouns to tell what he personally experienced, Rodney gives a rather complete step-by-step account of the activity. In her written response, Caryn inquires, "What is going to happen?" Her question asks him to go beyond what he did and to predict the outcome of their experiment. Rodney then writes the following prediction:

The washers will turn to crystals and put it in the sun because sun reflects on the washers.

Therefore, with Caryn's help he is able to offer a hypothesis. He also provides an explanation for his hypothesis. Hypothesis and explanation are two primary genres of scientific inquiry.

Other children begin with narrative accounts that can better be called stories because, like storytellers usually do, they select experiences or topics that they find particularly interesting (Labov 1970). Some might argue that science reports are not a narrative genre. However, given that children's first reading and writing experiences usually center on stories, it is not surprising that many children begin their science journals using this genre. Rodney's matter-of-fact account of what his group did contrasts with entries by other children who often tend to insert what we call "kid salient" details. These are aspects of the activity that appeal to, surprise, or entice children, aspects that are often emotionally charged. We use the term "kid salient" because adults or more experienced science writers would not mention such details, having learned that personal information is not usually included in science writing.

An example should help to illustrate this point. Colleen's entry describes the activity that involved popping one kernel of popcorn in a test tube. She writes:

> Today in science I popped popcorn. One popped, one did not pop. I had fun. I was not afraid to go near the fire. We all took turns. Everyone had fun. Everyone got along. The fire went out. Everyone cooperated. We had an argument. We solved the problems.

Colleen notes that her group completed the popcorn activity and tells the result of the experiment. In addition, she includes loosely associated details about how she felt and about group dynamics. It is obvious from her entry that the one aspect of the activity that impressed her most was "the fire" of the candle flame. With this kind of entry, Caryn has to read carefully and choose what she hopes the child will focus on. Colleen introduces several different topics, but Caryn chooses to pick up on Colleen's second sentence in which she tells of contrasting outcomes. Focusing on this discrepancy might be productive from the standpoint of the science content of the activity. Here's how the exchange continues:

> *Why do you think that one popped and one didn't?*
>
> We forgot to put foil.

Why do you think that the foil made a difference?

All the air came out of the test tube.

By calling Colleen's attention to the result of the experiment, namely that one popped and one didn't, Caryn is able to elicit Colleen's theory about what made the corn pop. Again, a child who starts with a narrative about the group activity ends by stating a theory, an important aspect of scientific thinking.

Another entry about the same activity also illustrates "kid salient" details. Mia begins her journal like this:

I put popcorn. The popcorn went up in the air. It splashed Mark T. and it splashed Carole and I got to be the timer. I like to be the timer.

Many of the kid salient details deal with accidents or spills, as here Mia writes about children being "splashed." Children often include affective information about what they enjoyed or disliked, as here Mia tells that she liked being the timer. The entry continues with Caryn's question:

What did you learn Mia?

I learned that if you put a popcorn kernel in the test tube it will pop like popcorn.

Why does it pop?

Cuz it has fire under the test tube.

In this case, Caryn uses a general question as a way to help Mia focus on an aspect of the scientific content that is interesting to her. When Mia offers her finding that her test tube kernel popped "like popcorn," Caryn is able to elicit an explanation of that phenomenon, which Mia attributes to the fire.

Caryn's question to Mia, "What did you learn?," a frequent one in wrap-up, is also often used in journal writing. Using this same question in both oral and written dialogue bridges the two practices and helps the children internalize the question. They quickly pick up on the fact that Caryn wants them to write about what they learned as well as what they did. Notice how Kyle begins his entry:

We learned how to observe and we used flames and test tubes. And we had to wear aprons and goggles.

Kyle's beginning shows a child reinterpreting the teacher's question. He is telling what he learned, but he highlights kid salient features, namely flames, test tubes, aprons, and goggles. The entry continues:

What did your group do? What did you find out?

We did things that we can change and it was a raisin.

What kind of change happened and why?

It got bigger and it changed color because there was air inside of the test tube.

What did the air do?

It evaporated.

Caryn's question prompts Kyle to tell the result of their experiment and he does say that they changed a raisin, but he gives no description of the change. Therefore, Caryn asks him to be more specific in telling about the change and to give an explanation for it. As with Mia, Caryn's questions support Kyle to offer an explanation for what happened rather than just to tell about it.

Procedures

Not all children begin with narratives; some try other forms. For instance, another common way that children write about their activities is by attempting to outline the procedures that they followed. In the next example, Jenny combines elements of a narrative with a more general description of how to do the activity. Again, notice that she has internalized Caryn's frequent question, "What did you learn?" She is also writing about the sugar crystal experiment that Rodney described:

I learned how to make crystals. The ingredients are 1/2 cup. You put it in a pan and then you wait until it boils. Then you put 1 3/4 cups of sugar into the pan and then I stir it until it dissolved. And then you put it in 2 big cups. And then you tie string onto a straw and a circle metal thing.

In Jenny's entry she is attempting to give general directions for "how to make crystals." Like Jenny, many children experiment with trying to provide a recipe-like procedure that someone could follow. It's obvious that she has not mastered this genre. For instance, for the most part she is telling someone else how to complete the activity, giving instructions using the second-person pronoun "you." Then, in the third sentence, she reintroduces her own experience: "I stir it until it dissolved." Thus, she combines the procedural recount of an oral report with this new written genre. Also note how she creatively makes herself understood although she does not have the technical vocabulary. She calls a washer a "circle metal thing." Here is the rest of her entry:

> *Why do you think crystals are going to grow?*
>
> Because water makes it grow and water makes plants grow.

Caryn's dialogue with Jenny relates to her first sentence in which she said that her instructions were about "how to make crystals." Caryn's "why" question prods Jenny to provide an explanation, one that involves a sensible and creative analogy: water makes plants grow, so it probably makes the crystals grow, too.

Direct Responses

The journal entries discussed so far are all good examples of children being supported to think and theorize about the science activities with the teacher's help. It should be pointed out, though, that some students have difficulty doing so. In fact, many children respond to the teacher's questions by indicating they can not answer. Here are two examples, both about the sugar crystal activity, that illustrate this point:

> In our group we had to put some water and some sugar and mixed stuff. And then we had to put the sugar water in two cups. And we had to put two washers and get some string and attached it to a stick. Then we had to put them and check it every day. The End.
>
> *What's going to happen and why?*
>
> They will turn into a crystal. I don't know Miss McCrohon.

In this entry, written by Carole, we see many features of the narrative genre including the traditional story ending, "The End." Although Carole is able to offer a prediction about the outcome of the experiment, she does not venture an explanation. So too, in Luke's entry:

> Today in our group we took some water and a pan and a little stove and a washer and a string and a stick and two cups. And we put it together and we have to wait a couple of days until it changes.

What kind of change is going to happen?

A crystal will grow on the water.

How does that happen?

I tried but I can't think what would happen.

Luke's entry shows another way that children use to begin writing, by listing the materials they used. This strategy was discussed in the last chapter as a way for reluctant reporters to begin in wrap-up. His entry is almost an inventory, ending with a very unspecific narrative clause that they "put it together." Like Carole, he provides his hypothesis, but declines to accept the challenge of figuring out why.

These entries show that there is a great degree of trust and ownership in the children's journals. This type of direct response indicates that children treat the teacher's questions as authentic ones that really seek their thinking, rather than as test questions requesting preformulated answers. Because they do not treat Caryn's questions as test questions, they are comfortable admitting that they have no answer to give, just as they are during wrap-up.

The following entry was also written by Carole. Her group did a balance activity in which they were supposed to balance paper clips on a straw that was suspended between blocks.

I learned nothing because we didn't get nothing done. Well anyhow we had to put two strong straws and put a pin in the middle and the sides with two pieces of wood. It was fun. Thank you Miss McCrohon for letting me be the facilitator. Bye bye journal. The end. OK.

Again, note the mixture of genres as Carole relates the procedure that her group followed, inserts a message to Caryn, and then concludes with "The end." As this entry continues, it becomes a clear example of a child's honesty, as evidenced by her response to Caryn's question.

Did you learn anything about how to get something to balance?

No.

Thus, an important aspect of dialogue journals is that they can provide a safe place for children to take risks, guess, and even acknowledge that they just don't know. As when Andy writes that "I can't explain how to convert cm into mm or mm into cm," it is important to allow children the freedom to make mistakes and admit when they have reasoned to the best of their ability and do not feel that they have the resources to go any further. Such honesty relates directly to the scientific habits of mind that Caryn and Patty are hoping to instill in their students. This information is also valuable for the teacher in planning the next logical lesson for the class.

"Real-world" Responses

Because children consider Caryn's questions to be authentic requests for information, their interpretation of what she is asking sometimes differs from what she expects to elicit from them. Whereas she is asking for school-based science thinking, they give what we call "real-world" answers. To understand what we mean by real-world answers, consider this entry written by Nancy after an activity in which the class flew kites and balloons:

> The kites would not fly because they were made of paper triangles. When I got home my mom said that Mr. B kept on saying it. One balloon went to New York. The End.

Nancy's narrative about the kites and balloons prompts Caryn to ask the following question:

You said that the kites didn't fly because they were made of paper triangles. Why?

Because they didn't have enough money to pay for the real ones.

Here, Caryn, as science teacher, means to ask, "Why didn't the kites fly?" Nancy, however, interprets the question as, "Why were the kites made of paper?" and provides an accurate response. At first, her answer seems funny and cute, but it is sensible, based on her understanding of the question, an understanding that better fits a conversational question than a science question in school.

Another example comes from Alan's journal, written about an activity in which two children sat on a seesaw, moving backward or forward until they balanced:

> Jerry had to move to the fulcrum because he was heavier.

Why?

> Because he eats more. If he eats more, he weighs more. When he moved closer to the fulcrum we balanced.

As in the previous example, there is a mismatch between what Caryn asks and what Alan answers. She wants to know why Jerry needed to move toward the fulcrum, and is attempting to prompt Alan to talk about the relationship between weight and distance in his group's experiment. Alan, however, obviously thinks that she wants to know why Jerry weighed more. Alan gives a very reasonable response to that question; it's just not the answer that Caryn expected.

Responses Focusing on Social Interaction

Children often begin their journal entries, like their reports, by talking about the social interaction that went on in their science groups. Often they write about problems in communicating or cooperating. An example comes from Andy's journal, written on the day he had experimented with putting different amounts of weight at various points on a balance scale. Note that he, too, anticipates Caryn's question "What did you learn?" and gives it an interpersonal slant:

> Me and Matt B. learned that it's very important to play your role. If a group member leaves, it's not a group anymore. If no one helps each other when they need help that person won't participate in your group.

In her response, Caryn makes her frequent question more specific in an effort to redirect Andy to the science content of the activity:

Did you learn anything scientific?

No!

Andy's reflection is an important one in terms of group dynamics. Furthermore, his honesty in saying that he learned nothing scientific ("No" with an exclamation point) shows that he has developed trust in the fact that Caryn wants to know what he really thinks. This entry, however, does not help Caryn, as a science teacher, in her effort to understand what Andy learned about the activity. As the dialogue continues, though, she is able to build upon the previous wrap-up discussion to probe for Andy's understanding of balance:

I thought during wrap-up you and I talked about the center of gravity.

If you have a scale that is not balanced you can move the thing you're weighing very close to the center of gravity. The center of gravity is the middle.

What will the center of gravity do?

It will balance the scale.

Why?

Because the scale is not quite balanced so it will make the side go down.

Andy's response demonstrates that he has an idea that the distance from the fulcrum matters when you want things to balance. Thus, through the written dialogue Caryn is able to redirect Andy's focus from interpersonal to more scientific concerns, and to uncover the fact that he has indeed learned something scientific.

Reflecting on the social dynamics of work in groups is an important part of journal writing that sometimes occupies the entire entry, just as it may be the focus of a reporter's whole turn. Occasionally, if the group does not cooperate, nothing can get done. Therefore, in such instances, Caryn uses dialogue as a way to help children be even more reflective about social issues. This example is written by Ross about an activity in which they converted centimeters to millimeters:

I learned that we did better working today. We made a ruler.

Why do you think you worked better?

Yesterday we didn't do nothing.

Why? What did you do different today? What made your group successful?

I did learn today but not yesterday.

Why did you get your work done today but not yesterday?

We cooperated.

Again, Ross begins with a spontaneous answer to the anticipated question "What did you learn?" and he offers a simple statement about what they did: "We made a ruler." However, Caryn does not ask about the activity per se, but rather about how the children worked together. Ross' group had a problem previously, so she wants him to think about how and why the group was more successful. The reflectiveness of this entry is not unusual among these children who have learned that their teacher truly wants them to write what they are learning about working together and about science.

Another kind of social entry is somewhat different in that it does not highlight problems, but rather attributes skills and abilities to others. These entries show the classroom emphasis on multiple abilities, that all children have something to contribute to the group, and that different students will have different strengths. Jenny writes about the activity in which they had to make a stable structure with straws, deciding how best to connect them. Her entry shows that the children worked cooperatively:

> When I was in group one my group made a tall structure. It was like a building. We worked all together. Kyle and me was good at ripping tape. Nancy was good at making squares. Missy was good at helping Nancy making squares. Carla was trying to make the top of the whole building. When we were building it stood. Everybody cooperated. Kyle and me are good at putting the straws up and taping.

Jenny's narrative obviously stresses interpersonal aspects of the activity, but it does so by emphasizing the skills that children in her group showed while working together. She also mentions their activity, that they made a tall building that stood. In addition, the reader can infer that it was made from squares and held together with tape.

As the entry continues, Caryn picks up on these references to the content of the activity:

Why did your structure stand?

The table was flat the rug was bumpy.

Did it stand on both?

It didn't stand on the rug. It stood on the table.

Caryn's question about why the structure stood is one that asks for Jenny's hypothesis about what would make it stable. Jenny's answer indicates that she understands the need for a proper base, since she states that it stood on the flat table, but not on the bumpy rug.

Responses That Indicate Problem Finding

One of the major benefits of using dialogue journals is that they allow the teacher to engage children not only in problem solving but also in problem finding. When children do the activities, they are very interested and involved in the doing but they are not necessarily taking time to reflect on how or why certain results occur. Dialoguing with the teacher can help children move beyond the actual process of completing hands-on science activities to reflect and begin to make sense of those activities. In the act of dialoging with students, teachers are able to problematize seemingly straightforward activities and outcomes. This type of teacher support of children's thinking takes place in whole-class wrap-up discussions, and also between the teacher and children while they are working on the activities. However, dialogue journals are personalized so that children can choose subjects or aspects of an activity that are interesting or puzzling to them and receive personal feedback and guidance from the teacher. Additionally, just as the dialogue of wrap-up can bring about insights, in dialogue journals it is often through the writing itself that problems are created and solved.

The next example is a dialogue journal exchange between Caryn and one of her students, Luke. This example is not easy to read, and may need to be read more than once. However, it is a good example of how children problem find and problem solve on-line. One reason that this example may be hard to read is that this child is struggling not only to find language suitable to express his ideas, but also he is discovering those ideas in the act of writing. What Luke is discovering through this written exchange with Caryn is that balance involves a relationship between distance and weight. His group has worked on the balance scale activity discussed above by Andy and also used in examples in other chapters. They used the plastic balance scale with pegs from which to hang ten-gram weights. Each peg is numbered, starting from the fulcrum on each side. Here is how he begins:

> When we were in group we put 2 grams on peg 3. The same on the right side. Then we put 4 grams on the left and 3 grams on the right. And we did other ones. And then I copied the pictures.

So far, he has written a recount of what his group did, describing much of the activity that occurred. He is very literal and complete in his retelling, even noting that he "copied the pictures," meaning that he drew in the weights on scales that were pictured on his activity card. What he doesn't write about are the outcomes of each balance activity and that's what Caryn asks:

> *What were your results?*

> Sometimes it balanced and sometimes it didn't. One time we put 4 grams on number one and 2 grams on number 3 and the left side weighed more than the right side and there was more grams on the right side.

Prompted by Caryn's question, Luke goes beyond the procedures he followed and states that they got varied results. He then describes the outcome of one problem in particular. When he says that "the left side weighed more than the right side," he actually means that the left side of the balance beam went down. In other words, the left side *acted* as though it weighed more even though there was more weight ("more grams") on the right. The fact that he chooses to describe this problem suggests this was a particularly interesting outcome for him. He presents details regarding the amount of weight and the location where weights were placed on the balance scale. However, his entry is still at the level of observation and description. Caryn asks another question:

> *Can you explain why that happened?*
>
> The higher the number is is [sic] the way it weighed more and that's weird too.

With this question, the dialogue moves from description to explanation. Luke offers an explanation that is clearly based on his prior description. It is not exactly clear what he means though, since he is using "number" to denote both weight and distance. In constructing his explanation he also says that the outcome he describes is "weird." The very fact that he calls this outcome "weird" shows that he is problem finding. He is considering what he just said and realizes that this outcome (greater distance acts as though it weighs more) is not what he expected. It violates his current theory that weight alone matters, thus it is "weird." Echoing his exact wording, Caryn then asks him to further explain what he means by the ambiguous statement "the higher the number." It is worth noting here that she uses this same strategy often if she is unable to figure out what children mean. When something is hard to paraphrase, as this statement is, she uses the child's own wording in her question to get them to tell more.

> *Why the higher the number it weighed more?*
>
> Because 3 is higher than 1 so it weighs more.

At this point it becomes clear that by saying "the higher the number," Luke is referring to the distance and not to the weight because he previously said that they put "2 grams on number 3." Taken as a whole this entry is a way for Luke to think through a surprising result. In addition, it allows him to entertain a new distinction: that balance is affected not only by weight but also by distance.

Responses That Anticipate Teacher Questions

Throughout this chapter and the last, we have talked about and shown examples of children using Caryn's frequent "What did you learn?" question as a framework for their own responses. The fact that they do so provides insight into the ways that anticipating the teacher's questions can enhance the quality of their journal responses. Consider the following two entries written by Julie. In the first she is describing an activity in which her group computed the perimeter of irregular shapes, in this case a star.

> I learned that a perimeter is something that you measure with.
>
> *How do you measure the perimeter of something?*
>
> You measure with something like a star. You take a ruler and put the ruler next to the star. Start by number 1 all the way down.
>
> *Then what?*
>
> Then you write it down.

Here, Caryn is trying to help Julie describe the complete procedure so that she can tell if Julie knows what perimeter is. Julie seems to be saying that they measured the sides of a star, and Caryn's question "Then what?" asks for the next step. Julie interprets this question literally, and notes that they wrote each measurement down.

Now look at her entry from the next day in which she writes about an activity that required children in her group to find symmetrical and asymmetrical shapes.

> I learned that if you cut a computer it will be asymmetrical. Then you write it down.
>
> *Can you explain symmetry and asymmetry?*
>
> OK. Asymmetrical is if you cut something in half it is different. The opposite of symmetrical.

Note that in her first independent turn Julie anticipates Caryn's "Then what?" question by adding the very same information that she included only after the teacher's prompt on the day before: "Then you write it down."

Another example shows that children become accustomed to Caryn's questions. Nancy was writing about an activity in which they experimented with parachutes of different sizes:

> The little parachute flew faster than the other one. Because when one's smaller it goes faster and the big ones go slow. The end.

Here Nancy tells about what she observed and gives a beginning explanation for the fact that the small parachute fell faster. She includes the narrative closure "The end." However, this is not the end of her entry because on the next line she writes, "Ms. McCrohon Questions." Nancy literally makes a place for her teacher to enter the conversation, and Caryn does so in the following way:

> Ms. McCrohon Questions.
>
> *Why does the big one go slower?*
>
> Because it has more air pressure.
>
> *What does that mean?*
>
> It means some thing is air pressure.
>
> *Could you explain what you think air pressure is?*
>
> I think it is when some air comes out of something.

Responses That Show Frustration: Knowing When Enough Is Enough

Although Nancy does not have a clear idea of what air pressure is, she is willing to continue the conversation and give a try at a definition. There are some children, however, who become somewhat frustrated with repeated questions. An example is from an entry written by Julie. It describes an activity in which her group had to balance objects on a pegboard, experimenting with placement and weight:

> We learned that it is easy to balance.
>
> *That does not tell me anything scientific.*
>
> We had a pegboard and we balanced stuff.
>
> *What happened?*
>
> Our group did not listen very well!
>
> *Tell me about the balancing activity.*
>
> OK. We had a pegboard and we put different stuff on it. One worked but John was not listening! I told you everything I did with the pegboard!

This entry is a complicated mixture of many things. First, it starts as a response to the question "What did you learn?" By this point in the year, the class has discussed the idea that children should write about the science content, so Caryn reminds Julie about this in her first response. In reply, Julie tells a bit about their procedure, and includes interpersonal information about the group in her next turn. What is notable here is

Julie's last sentence which obviously is a frustrated attempt to ward off anticipated further questions.

An entry written by Christine also indicates a child's frustration. Her group worked on an activity in which they had to build a tall and sturdy structure with straws, connecting them with pins.

> Balance is if you build a building and it stands up. Structure is building stuff like a building. We used pins and straws and tried to get it to balance. The end.

Christine begins her entry with definitions of balance and structure followed by a simple narrative sentence about what her group did. She concludes with "The end." The entry continues with Caryn's question:

> *How do things balance?*
>
> By making it on the same sides even.

So far, so good. Caryn asks for a further explanation about balance and Christine elaborates on her initial idea, that is, a building stands up because it is even on both sides. Then Caryn presses her to be more explicit:

> *What do you mean, make it the same? Make what the same?*
>
> Like if one side was a square and the other side was a circle then it would fall because it would be crooked.
>
> *What about the weight?*
>
> The circle side would be 100 and the square side would be 200.
>
> *I don't understand.*
>
> Because when they built it they made it that way.

As this exchange continues, Christine's responses become farther removed from her own experience with the building activity. It is difficult to pinpoint the exact source of Christine's frustration. However, Caryn now thinks that her question "What about the weight?" does not sufficiently build on what Christine is trying to say because Christine mentions nothing about weight. In retrospect, Caryn would have stopped after Christine's response about the square side and the circle side, from which a reader can infer that she considers symmetry important for balancing a building.

Some Guidelines for Using Dialogue Journals in Science

The point of dialoging with children is to support them to do more than they can on their own (Vygotsky 1978), yet it is important to appreciate and try to understand children's independent beginnings. There is no one right or wrong response in a journal because each entry is unique; we cannot provide a list of questions that will work for all children.

Each child's entry has to be responded to on-line by Caryn, who accepts whatever a child writes as an initial entry, even if it is very brief or hard for her to understand. She never sends a child back to try again, nor does she tell anyone that an entry is not good enough. She builds on what her students offer as their best initial try. This acceptance creates an atmosphere of trust that enables children with very different abilities to enter into the activity. It also allows children to write something, however brief, about activities that they didn't understand, or things that did not go well. Again, there is an obvious comparison to wrap-up discussions in which reporters' initial turns are always accepted and built upon.

General Guidelines

Children are encouraged to write and spell as best they can, and, not surprisingly, they display a wide range of control over the conventions of written language. If children's writing is hard to decipher because of letter formation or early phonetic spelling, they are asked to read their entry aloud so that it can be understood. For these same children, Caryn says her words aloud as she writes them so that struggling readers will understand her questions.

Children are also free to express themselves as best they can. Caryn does not require technical language or specific vocabulary when they are describing their activities. Recall the entry where Jenny called a washer a "circle metal thing." Caryn knows the materials that the children used and therefore knew what Jenny meant. Clarification was not necessary for them to communicate. Using children's exact words can also be an effective strategy when Caryn does not fully understand what they mean. Remember that this was the case when Luke was writing about the balance scale problem and used the phrase "the higher the number," which was ambiguous whether he was referring to weight or distance.

On the other hand, there are some words and concepts that receive a lot of attention in certain science units. For instance, when learning about measuring shapes, children worked with diameter and circumference. Therefore, these words become the object of Caryn's questions in response to the activities that involve measuring circles. Caryn also is careful about modeling vocabulary, spelling, and other conventions, valuing journal writing as a literacy event as well as an opportunity for science learning.

It's also true that sometimes a child will use a technical term, but have little understanding of its meaning. Witness Kyle's entry about an activity in which his group explored the concepts of longitude and latitude using an orange:

> Latitude is a circle line that goes around the globe. Longitude goes north to south. The orange did not have any latitude.

Kyle uses scientific vocabulary and defines longitude. Knowing the activity, Caryn can also infer that he understands longitude because he is correct that the orange only has lines dividing its sections, not any that go across. This is how the entry continues:

> *Why do you think that there are latitude and longitude lines on a globe or a map?*
>
> Because I saw them on a globe.
>
> *Why are they even on a map or a globe?*
>
> It tells how many degrees there are.

Although Kyle's answer to Caryn's first question probably falls into the real-world category as discussed earlier in this chapter, his response to her follow-up question sounds very scientific, including the technical term "degrees." Caryn then asks one final question:

> *What do you mean by degrees?*
>
> Degrees tell how hot or cold.

Obviously, Kyle's confusion is understandable, and he knows the most common meaning of the word degrees. His use of the term in this context, however, though it sounds good on the surface, does not represent a deep understanding of the concepts that he is writing about. Later in the book we will discuss how journals can be used for assessment, and this is a good example to keep in mind.

Teacher Decisions

The hardest part for the teacher is that there are many decisions to be made, and, because these journals are "written conversations," the decisions must be made quickly. After all, while Caryn is thinking, there is a child standing waiting for her response. Worse, there may even be a growing line of children awaiting their turns.

Is there something to ask that will focus them on the underlying important concepts? The first decision is choosing which part of a child's entry to build on. Luckily, this dilemma is most easily solved at the beginning of the year when children may only write one sentence or idea. Obviously, that one thought is what the teacher must react to, given the basic premise of accepting what the child initially offers. However, as the year goes on, students' entries get longer and often they will mention several ideas in their initial turn. When this happens, the decision about which part is most important ideally hinges on the teacher's knowledge of the scientific "big idea" that underlies the activity and the unit as a whole.

Is there something to ask that will focus them on the particulars of how they did their experiment? With open-ended science activities conducted by groups of young children, the decision about what to build on may also be made based upon the teacher's knowledge of what the group did. The difference here is that children sometimes do not do the experiment exactly as they are supposed to, and their most important insights may come as a result of what they did differently.

Is there something to ask about what they accomplished with their experiment, or will it be more productive to focus their attention on the importance of group cooperation? Another important decision is whether to concentrate on the social interaction mentioned in an entry or to ignore that part and try for the science. This is obviously a judgment call. Recall the examples that we used to illustrate children's emphasis on interpersonal aspects of their groupwork. In some, Caryn writes back with this same emphasis; in others she asks a science question. Caryn usually will ask about science if there is any kernel of science content in what the child writes. Sometimes, even though they dwell entirely on social issues, she knows from observing the groups that they did indeed work on their experiments. It may be, too, that she knows this from what they mention in the wrap-up discussion. Again, it's important to note that she fully accepts social entries without devaluing what the child has to say. Often, the interaction was the most important part of the science lesson for that day.

Is there another fruitful question to ask, or has the child had enough? The final decision is when to stop. Using journals as written conversation can be time consuming, since it has to be done interactively with the children during class time. Caryn takes advantage of the day's natural boundaries of lunch time or dismissal to signal that time is up for that day. However, within the time allotted, the teacher must still decide whether to pursue questioning with a child, or to stop and congratulate her on a job well done. As was exemplified by the entries that show children's frustration, the teacher can ask one or two questions too many, and Caryn admits that she does so occasionally. To remedy this situation, there is no substitute for simply knowing the children. Some will welcome multiple challenges, others may struggle to answer a single question.

When a teacher knows her students well enough, she will be able to interpret remarks like the one by Andy with which we began this chapter. When some children say "No more challenges," they are asking for relief; when Andy said it, he was playfully encouraging Caryn to ask yet another question.

6 *Making Connections*

LUKE: **It was like mushy, like Gak.**

CARYN: **Gak? What's Gak?**

LUKE: **It's like slime. Nickelodeon Gak. My sister got it.**

CARYN: **Oh** *(Laughs)* **like Gak! Well that's a comparison.**

As teachers encourage children to choose their own topics for writing, or to respond personally to literature, more and more students are bringing their lives into the classroom, and in the process enriching the learning community. In the excerpt quoted above, Luke is doing just that: trying to make sense of new experiences by relating them to what he already knows while introducing his teacher to a new idea at the same time. However, we have found that connections like this do not just happen. Children often do not see school science as connected to their out-of-school experiences. Analogies like the one that Luke made come about because Patty and Caryn have made an effort to help their students see and make connections, especially during wrap-up and journal writing, when they, as teachers, have a chance to ask questions and promote certain types of thinking.

Maureen's Story

Early in the first year of our collaboration, I visited Caryn and Patty's classrooms at least once a week. While the kids were in their groups, I walked around with my notebook, and then I usually took a place in the back of the room during wrap-up when I would switch on my tape recorder and concentrate on what was being said. At the very beginning, my intent was to become aware of what was going on and to be around enough that the teachers and children were comfortable having me there. During these early visits, I often wondered what I would find from a research perspective and what I might eventually write about. So, as I began to watch, tape, and transcribe, I also began to speculate about possible topics.

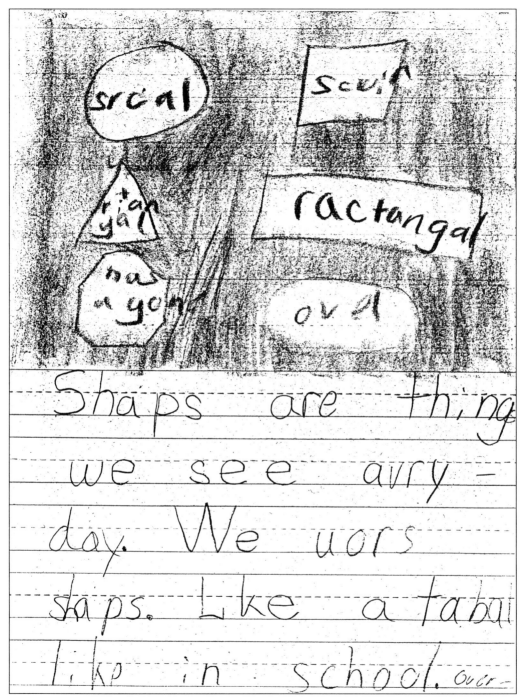

6–1 Christine's journal: "Shapes are things we see everyday"

During one of my first observations, I recorded the following conversation that took place in Patty's room during wrap-up. Patty and Lauren were discussing an activity in which children heat a raisin in a test tube over a flame, noting any changes that they observe.

PATTY: Ohhh. Do you think that heat changes something Lauren? How do you think it changed it?

LAUREN: Because it's just . . . just like . . . just like soup cuz first it's all hard . . . like spaghetti and then when you boil it just like soup. When the raisin gets cooked and boiled . . . It's just like soup when then circles are . . . it's just like they're hard and then when you boil em they get all mushy. And it's like that.

Lauren made an extended and very appropriate analogy between what took place when she heated the raisin and what happens when you make dehydrated soup. Patty told the class that she considered Lauren's statement to be "very interesting and very important." I certainly agreed, as did her classmates who showed a great deal of interest. I was excited because I know that analogies are important in science and I thought that I might be able to study and write about the types of comparisons the children made.

In another example, Lauren first explained to the class that a structure built by her group did not stand on its own. A classmate then asked a question:

JOY: Why doesn't it stand up?

KRISTA: Because it's not straight.

LAUREN: It's like the crooked old man in the story. This is the crooked old man's house.

In her reply, Lauren alluded to a familiar rhyme as she elaborated on Krista's explanation about why the building could not stand on its own. This, too, was an apt connection that delighted her audience.

Having heard these two examples early in the year, I was intrigued. I thought that maybe I could study the kinds of comparisons that children make, comparisons between novel experiences that happen in their science activities and things with which they were already familiar. I decided that, as I transcribed, I would make special note of such instances. In the abstract, it was a good idea, but there was not much to take note of because the examples that I cite above are exceptions. Across the entire year in both classes, such comparisons hardly ever happened.

It's as though students considered their experiences in the classroom to be separate from their lives outside. The children as a group treated wrap-up as a time and place to talk only about their experiences in science groups, without reference to other similar experiences, treating it as a bounded space. At the time we were a bit surprised, but we are not alone in this observation. According to Neil Mercer (1991) in a paper entitled "Putting Context into Oracy,"

> The notion that the proper business of the lesson centers on what is "done" in class, rather than by reference to the wider world, appears to be understood by the pupils themselves. They appear to operate within a ground rule to the effect that, if a teacher asks a question related to the work done in class, then the answer is to be found in what the lesson actually covered. (127)

Similarly, James Wertsch (1991) claims:

> An underlying assumption of most sessions of formal instruction is that one must not introduce or presuppose information from "outside" the classroom unless specifically invited to do so. It is as if an invisible barrier has been placed around the topical "space" that is eligible for discussion. (127)

Evidently something about the contexts in both classrooms the first year had created this "invisible barrier," yet we believe that children learn best when they can make meaningful connections that can help them understand new things in light of what they already know. In fact, making connections is explicitly mentioned as one of the "habits of mind" in *Benchmarks for Science Literacy* (1993), which states: "Students should be able to connect one idea with another and use it in thinking about new situations and in problem solving" (283). Armed with the knowledge that connections did not just happen in her class, during the next year Caryn made a concerted effort to work on making them happen.

Real-world Connections

The connections that we discussed above are what we call "real-world" connections. It is this type of connection that Caryn concentrated on during the year that followed our discovery that students very infrequently made such connections on their own. She often would ask the children about the "real world." The example that follows is from a unit in which the class had been doing activities involving shapes and learning how to find perimeter. Caryn wants them to understand that this is not just a school activity, but that finding perimeter is a useful skill in life outside of the classroom. A dialogue journal entry written by Kyle, however, shows that this process is not always easy:

> I learned about perimeter. Perimeter means you measure around the sides of the shape. But you can use a geo board.
>
> *What do you do after you get the measurements for each side?*
>
> You add the numbers together.
>
> *Why do we use perimeter? Real world?*
>
> I don't know.

Caryn's rather abbreviated question, where she tacks on the words "real world," shows that the class has talked about this type of connection before. They had become accustomed to her asking the question, but they were not yet able to answer with any specificity. In this example it's probably not the case that Kyle knows the connections but is not using them. Rather, most likely at seven years old he has never thought about finding perimeter as a useful process outside of school.

Therefore, Caryn set out to promote real-world connections by making the children aware of the relevance of what they are being asked to do. In the following example Caryn is developing a very explicit connection using an actual object to give them concrete experience with perimeter. That day, Ramone brought in a toy workbench/tool set which consisted of a variety of shapes that fit into holes cut to match.

MATT: A perimeter is measuring maybe up, down, sideways.

CARYN: What if you had a square?

MARK: If you had a square it would . . .

MATT: *(Interrupts)* If you could draw a square right here then you could measure down, sideways, up, and over. That's what a perimeter is.

CARYN: It's the outside of a shape.

MARK: Right.

CARYN: Because if we had to . . . You know the toy that Ramone brought in, where you bang the shapes into, was it . . .

MARK: *(Interrupts)* Like a tool set.

CARYN: A tool set. Were some of the shapes you have to bang squares?

MARK: Yeah.

RAMONE: Yeah.

CARYN: Go get it for me, Ramone. *(Ramone gets the toy)* Thanks Ramone. Let me see if this is what I was talking about. Well, this [a cylinder]. . . this might come in handy when we talk about the circumference. But look at this. This happens to be something that this rectangle will fit right through. See this? They, the people that made these shapes, figured that they needed a container and it would be easier if you could just keep the cover on and slip it through. Right? How do you think that they came up with how big this should be? Rodney?

RODNEY: They probably first, they made like one of these, then they put it in the middle, and decided the shape, do it around it, like sawed around it.

RAMONE: *(Very hesitant)* I don't know . . . I don't know.

Rodney's theory is that the rectangular hole was made by tracing around the shape that needed to fit into it. This theory is most likely based on his experience. He knows that you can reproduce a shape by tracing because he has traced things before. He may also know that the resulting image is slightly larger than the object. Caryn restates his theory both to be sure she understands and to make it clearer for the class. She goes on to collect other views:

CARYN: You think they traced it? I think someone else has an idea. Ramone.

RAMONE: I think that . . . can I show you up there?

CARYN: Sure.

RAMONE: I think they took this and like put this in the middle. There's enough room for it to slip through, so they make it a teeny bit wider, so it can slip back and forth.

CARYN: Um-hm. Matt, did you have any suggestions?

MATT: I think they took a big metal thing that like pushed this through cuz maybe it was stuck on this that was a little wider so it just pushed the plastic up a little.

These theories are not really explanations of how they created a hole that's the right size; they deal simply with how a hole was made. Caryn directs the conversation back to the problem: how they made it the proper size.

CARYN: What if I told you that is not what happened. They didn't punch anything, they didn't punch this through. Is there another way they could have found out how big to make this? Julie?

JULIE: They could have measured this then they like could like here they could measured here.

CARYN: You're right, Julie.

ANDY: Measured the di-, no what's that? Measured the perimeter.

CARYN: They could have measured the perimeter of this shape and they could have taken their measurements and decided they needed to make it a little wider, so they were able to get an accurate measurement.

MARK: Right.

CARYN: That's why sometimes we have perimeter to measure the outside of the shape.

In this example, the children are engaged in trying to figure out how the toy was made. Their first suggestions involve using the actual objects to determine the size of the holes, but then Julie mentions measuring and Andy makes the connection to the perimeter activity that they had just done.

Another example comes from a cold day in January, when the children were doing measurement activities. Their task was to measure objects in the room with centimeter rulers, using both centimeters and millimeters to get as accurate a measurement as possible. Formerly, they had only rounded to the nearest centimeter:

CARYN: What about . . . what about the points? Remember when we had 10.3? Do you know why the .3 was there? Does anyone know? Luke?

LUKE: I think it because . . . um . . . why was it there?

CARYN: Yeah why did we have to use points? Why was it 10.3 centimeters?

LUKE: Cuz some of the millimeters were hanging off.

CARYN: That's right. Some of the millimeters were hanging off. It was ten centimeters plus three extra millimeters so it was 10.3. It's a more accurate way of measuring. Because if we try to put a window in a place that was 10.3 centimeters but we only measure ten . . . we're going to be three millimeters short. We're going to get air through that window aren't we? It's going to be cold. That's why it needs to be accurate.

In this case, Luke cannot explain why they needed to use the "point three" which is the way that they represent the millimeter portion of their measurement. In fact, for most of the children, this level of precision was either too difficult or too exact. They either couldn't do it or couldn't figure out why it would be worth the trouble. Caryn's reference to the window is a very concrete illustration of why you would want an accurate measurement to keep out the wintry wind. Again, it is worth noting that she uses the child's language in her response by saying that the "millimeters were hanging off," showing that she understands and accepts his explanation.

Based on experiences like these in which Caryn clearly demonstrates how to connect what they learn in science to the real world, children will begin to relate novel experiences to what they already know about without being prompted. This is especially true when they are trying to define words to explain new concepts. In the following example, Ramone does a great job of explaining what dissolving means. The children have dissolved an antacid tablet in a test tube of water and many of them have said that it disappeared. You will notice here that disappearing and dissolving seem to be used interchangeably by both Caryn and Ramone. By the end, though, Ramone distinguishes between the two phenomena and he comes to this understanding by talking about how a vitamin pill dissolves in your mouth:

CARYN: Ramone, did your antacid dissolve?

RAMONE: I don't know.

CARYN: Do you know what dissolving is?

RAMONE: Yes.

CARYN: And what is it?

RAMONE: It's when something there . . . let's say you took a vitamin. You sticked it into your mouth. You're sucking on it and when you took it out it was small. Then you put it back in. Then when you thought it was still in there you looked to take it out and nothing was there, was in there.

When asked if the antacid dissolved, Ramone says that he doesn't know, not because he doesn't know what dissolving means, but because his definition does not include what the antacid did. According to the children, it first "exploded" and then "disappeared." Ramone defines dissolving with the example of a vitamin pill dissolving in his mouth. As the conversation continues, Caryn helps him to expand his definition to include the new experience. Note that at the beginning of this exchange Caryn says "disappeared," the term that the children have been using.

CARYN: It was gone. It kinda disappeared? Is there something in your mouth that makes it disappear?

RAMONE: Well, yeah.

CARYN: What's in your mouth? Is your mouth dry or wet?

RAMONE: Wet, but the way it dissolved is a special kind of spit from underneath your tongue and it gets at the food that you're chewing or you're sucking and makes it dissolve or either a chew.

CARYN: So you think it . . . spit is wet, right? Is spit wet, Ramone? Is spit wet?

RAMONE: Yes.

CARYN: Is water wet?

RAMONE: Yes.

CARYN: Did the same thing happen to your antacid that happened to your vitamin?

RAMONE: Well, that I don't know.

CARYN: I mean, obviously your vitamins don't um explode, but they dissolve you said.

RAMONE: Yeah?

CARYN: And was . . . did could you see your antacid tablet after you poured the water in?

RAMONE: Uh no.

CARYN: And the bubbles stopped?

RAMONE: Uh no.

CARYN: So did it dissolve?

RAMONE: Yeah.

CARYN: Where'd it go?

RAMONE: Disappeared.

CARYN: It disappeared?

RAMONE: But it's still in there.

CARYN: But it's still in there. How'd you know it was still in there?

RAMONE: Well, that is a hard question but—*(Pause)*.

CARYN: What sense could you use? You can't see it. How else would you tell? What sense could you use? Your hearing, tasting, touching, smelling. Which one could you use to see it was still in?

RAMONE: Smelling or taste, I don't know.

CARYN: That's right, smelling or tasting.

When Ramone agrees that the pill dissolved and claims that it disappeared, Caryn then questions its disappearance and he asserts "But it's still in there," knowing that when you take a vitamin it's still in your body. He clearly has both expressed and expanded his understanding of dissolving.

In another example, Matt uses his knowledge of a familiar word to define octagon.

MATT: Ms. McCrohon I have . . . I have a . . . I don't really have a question, but I think I know why they call the shape that starts with an "o" I think.

CARYN: Octagon? Octahedron?

MATT: Yeah, I think I know why they call it that.

CARYN: Why?

MATT: Because it has eight sides. An octagon has eight sides, and an octopus has eight arms.

Here, Matt is relating an unfamiliar term (octagon) to something that he knows about (an octopus) and has explained why they have the same prefix.

In a journal entry, Cora also defined a term by using something familiar:

I take gymnastics and if you go on the balance beam you have to balance. Balance means to be equal.

Using real-world knowledge is also evident in group theory building as evidenced by another example. One group of children has done the popcorn activity while another has heated the raisin. The reporter from the popcorn group has related their observation that there is "juice" in the test tube (their word for condensation on the sides). The fact that there is moisture inside the popcorn kernel is a crucial fact for understanding how and why it pops, so the moisture is well worth discussing at length. The children have stated that the popcorn, before heating, is "bone dry," and they have decided that the moisture in the test tube in which they heated a raisin is "raisin juice," and that's the explanation to which Andy refers at the beginning when he questions the reporter:

ANDY: Did you add like water or oil into the thing? Then it probably must have been raisin juice if you didn't add anything else.

CARYN: But what I'm trying to prove is that the test tube with the popcorn that's bone dry inside had the same liquid on the inside of the test tube.

CHILD: It might have been different kind . . . kind of liquid.

CHILD: Maybe it was oil.

CARYN: What if I told you it was the same thing?

CHILD: Then that's . . . strange.

CARYN: What kind of an explanation could we have?

ANDY: Maybe it's . . . the same thing.

JOE: Maybe it's from the fire.

ANDY: Yeah maybe it's from the fire.

In trying to connect the two activities, Caryn points out to the children that the popcorn test tube and the raisin test tube seem to have the same liquid in them. She is hoping that the children will conclude that the liquid cannot be raisin juice. One child voices an opinion that seems to be shared by others, saying "That's strange." Several children offer theories about how the moisture got there, each one introducing an alternative with "Maybe it's . . ." Caryn then explicitly states, "Then there should be some sort of explanation for how that liquid got inside the test tube when it wasn't there to begin with," and the conversation continues:

ANDY: Maybe the fire made like probably sweat . . . sweat kind of like.

CARYN: Sweat? Luke?

LUKE: Sometimes when I go in the shower if it's on too long you can look in the mirror in the bathroom and it's all steamed up.

CARYN: Oh that's . . . that's a good observation Luke made. Did you hear what Luke said? He said that sometimes . . . when you go into the bathroom to take a shower or a bath and it's really hot water what happens?

CHILD: It's steamy.

CARYN: It's steamy. What does that steam do to your bathroom mirror?

DINA: It makes it wet.

CARYN: It makes it wet. Well let's think about that and inside the test tube what might that be? Mia?

MIA: Well . . . *(Long pause)*.

ANDY: Steam?

Using Luke's observational connection to what happens when he takes a shower, Andy comes up with the suggestion that it's steam. Caryn then proposes an experiment that will provide a further link with their personal experiences.

CARYN: Could be steam. Next time you take a bath or a shower go over to your mirror afterwards and wipe you fingers down it.

ALYCIA: That's what I do.

CARYN: See what comes off on your fingers. You tell me if you think it's oil or if it's water. You tell me what you think it is. I want to hear those answers. Dina thank you for raising.

DINA: Um I wipe my hand on the glass . . . on my mirror all the time and nothin . . . and nothin comes on my fingers.

CARYN: Do you have a fan in your bathroom?

DINA: No.

CARYN: No.

ANDY: I get wet hands whenever I do it.

CHILD: I get hot ones.

CARYN: Do you take a bath or a shower?

CHILD: Sometimes a bath, sometimes a shower.

CARYN: I think it happens more when you take a shower than when you take a bath.

After Caryn suggests testing the steam on the bathroom mirror as an at-home experiment, Dina makes another connection:

Sometimes when you eat you see like smoke coming up from . . . from your plate cuz when it was on the um . . . inside the pan so long on the fire.

Dina has drawn a parallel between steam on the bathroom mirror and steam in food. Luke later picks up this train of thought.

LUKE: Like before when I was eating and I had something real real hot I had a glass cup right near the plate.

CARYN: Um-hm.

LUKE: And like after a while I was letting it cool off . . . it was steamy.

CARYN: You had some liquid on the inside of it?

LUKE: No on the outside.

CARYN: On the outside of it?

CHILD: Yeah. That's what always happens when I have a hot dinner.

As you can tell, the children have had many relevant experiences with steam, whether taking a hot shower or watching pots on the stove or even observing hot food on their plates. This kind of discussion can be extremely productive as a way for them to relate the moisture on the popcorn test tube to the kinds of moisture that they have already experienced as examples of steam. The fact that there is moisture inside the kernel is key to understanding why it pops, and it is not evident from examining the seemingly dry kernel that it is capable of forming steam. With the three variables of heat, moisture, and steam, they may be able to learn how the kernel pops in a much more meaningful way than simply being told.

In the following example, Caryn is trying to help the children make the distinction between polygons as "flat shapes" and polyhedra as three dimensional shapes. The class has already come up with one difference: you can kick a polyhedron. They tested this theory by kicking a ball around the room and then trying to kick a circle that was cut from a piece of paper.

CARYN: Do you guys know the candy bar, what's it called? It's a sq-, oh a Chunky bar? The candy bar is Chunky?

DINA: Looks like a ball.

CARYN: No doesn't it kind of look like a, uh, almost like a cube but like in a trapezoid kind of shape.

CHILD: Jolly Rancher?

CARYN: What? A Jolly Rancher? Oh, a Jolly Rancher for example is a cube right, well, it's a rectangular kind of cube right? Is a Jolly Rancher candy hollow inside or is it solid?

CLASS: Solid.

CARYN: It's solid. Is it a polyhedron? *(Many children say Yes, Yeah, No, Yeah.)*

RAMONE: You can kick a Jolly Rancher around this whole room Ms. McCrohon.

CHILD: It's too little.

ANGEL: But you still could.

RAMONE: If you made a huge one the size of a soccer ball then you could.

In this conversation so far, you can see that Caryn is trying to make a real-world connection using her own frame of reference, a Chunky bar. The children don't pick up on her idea, but rather offer one of their own, a Jolly Rancher, a type of hard candy that's shaped like a cubed rectangle. They then go on to debate whether this small candy will pass the "kick test."

When children begin to take ownership of making connections, as in the example above, they often use comparisons that are apt but unusual. A favorite example is when they were doing the popcorn experiment, comparing the kernel before and after. A child from a group that had already done the activity remarked to the reporter that "the popcorn kernel looked like George Washington with white hair." As soon as he said this, quite a few children chimed in with "Yeah." The comparison obviously made sense to them. We also had to admit that, when we viewed it from the right angle, we could conjure up a white colonial hairdo.

Connections Between Activities

A second type of connection follows logically from the design of the Complex Instruction science program that Patty and Caryn use. Each unit is constructed with a "Big Idea," or theme, to which all the activities relate. Although the tasks are not sequenced, and can be done in any order, what children learn from one activity (whether they do that activity or hear about it from classmates during wrap-up) enhances their learning about the others, building upon the conceptual redundancy that is part of the design. In addition, their interest is also piqued before they do a certain activity because they anticipate doing it themselves after hearing about it from others. After they have done it, they like to compare their results and experiences with those of the group that is reporting. We notice that their questions often increase and improve after they have done activities themselves because they have first-hand experiences upon which to base them.

As we said earlier, the structure of the Complex Instruction system is based on different groups of children rotating through a series of activities for several days. For instance, during one week, five activities in a unit are done, each by a different group of children on a given day. At the end of the week, all five groups of children will have done each activity. The popcorn activity, for example, would be done on five successive days by Groups 1–5. For wrap-up, this rotation means that there will be five reports about the popcorn activity across the five days of the unit. On the first day, the child who reports about the popcorn will be the first to present that activity. On the next day, the reporter who describes the popcorn will have heard one report about it. On the third day, that reporter will have heard two other children talk, and so on.

This rotation also affects the knowledge of the audience. For instance, suppose that five children in Group 1 did the popcorn activity on the first day. When their reporter reports, only the other four members of that group have insider knowledge about that task as they listen to the first report about it. The next day, the activity rotates to Group 2, so that when their reporter reports, members of both Groups 1 and 2 will have done the activity. Thus, the audience for a report changes daily, with a larger number of children having done each activity as the unit progresses. When the class assembles for wrap-up on the last day, all children should be familiar with all activities, having been in each group and heard four prior reports about it. In the first year of using this method, the teachers-as-audience also changed because on the first day they had no experience with children doing the activity, and they too gained familiarity as the unit unfolded, both from hearing multiple reports and monitoring different groups. Even now, since the activities are so open-ended, the teachers' stance as audience member still is modified across the days of a unit.

At the beginning we expected that children would give more sophisticated reports as the unit progressed because students had more models and greater knowledge. As we showed in Chapter 4, many of these young children had a great deal of trouble reporting and we did not see vast differences in reports across days. However, when we read and reread the transcripts, and began to do some very careful analysis, we noticed connections, connections that can be seen as what is called "intertextuality" or links between the texts of reports.

Intertextuality is often talked about with reference to reading-writing connections, as a way to think about how the books that children read influence the texts that they write (Cairney 1990). Other teachers and researchers have looked at intertextuality in literature circles, noting how response and interpretation are enriched by connections to other literary works (Short 1986). We use the notion of intertextuality as a tool to understand the connections that children make in their reports as they engage in reasoning episodes with Caryn and Patty. A quote from the Russian linguist Bakhtin is also relevant here:

> The living utterance, having taken meaning and shape at a particular historical moment in a socially specific environment, cannot fail to brush up against thousands of living dialogic threads, woven by socio-ideological consciousness around the given object of an utterance; it cannot fail to become an active participant in social dialogue. (1981, 276)

Each report in each wrap-up occurs in a series of such discussions that are interconnected within the recurring practices of the classroom community. Therefore, based on Bakhtin's theory, it is reasonable to assume that any wrap-up will be "in social dialogue" with other wrap-ups that have occurred or have yet to take place. That is, they will be intertextual. This assumption raises the question of how reports build on each other given that children have heard other reporters talk about their activities on previous days.

Procedural Links Across a Unit

At the second-grade level, the very process of doing activities often presents a challenge. Children have to learn to carefully manipulate, measure, pour, and perform other actions that are key to their obtaining results. One way that meaningful connections are made across days is in the evolution of procedural knowledge. When Ross got up to report about his activity in which they first had to balance one straw by placing it perpendicular to another and then balance paper clips on the upper straw, he claimed that "Today was very better than yesterday." Then there is short discussion about how this activity fit in with others that they had done:

CARYN: Can you compare any of the stuff that you did with any of the groups that have come up today? Did you do anything similar?

ROSS: Yeah. We balanced.

CARYN: You balanced. Was everything always the same weight?

ROSS: Nnnno not always.

CARYN: And you still got them to balance?

ROSS: Yeah.

CARYN: So compare that to one of the other groups. Did you do something that's the same thing that the other groups did?

ROSS: Yeah.

CARYN: What?

ROSS: That um the um the most um in one.

CARYN: Heavier?

ROSS: Yeah. The heavier part was in more so . . .

As Caryn and Ross are having this exchange about weight and distance, Matt interrupts with the following:

MATT: Hey Ross. I know . . . I know one thing.

ROSS: What?

MATT: I know one thing that you didn't do that our group um did yesterday.

CHILD: What?

MATT: Mess up. You didn't mess up on the straws.

MARK: Well that's one thing.

ROSS: We didn't mess up.

MATT: I know that's what I'm saying. We did.

CARYN: But they learned from your mistake.

MATT: I know.

On the day before Matt's group had a hard time getting the balance to function. As a result they had nothing to report except their problems, which they related to the group. Obviously Ross and his collaborators had been listening because they "didn't mess up on the straws." Matt not only took responsibility for the previous mistake, but also praised Ross' group for learning from it. The fact that Ross and his group gained practical information and advice from the prior report meant that it had a beneficial experience that helped Ross to think and talk about the content of the activity.

This process of learning procedures from previous groups is sometimes very explicit, especially when Caryn asks each group if they have any advice for those who will do their activity next. This practice came about because it was evident that children had learned helpful procedures, but they did not necessarily make them public. Andy's journal entry shows this:

In my group I learned nothing. Our group tried to weigh things but the scale could not balance.

Didn't you figure out a way for the scale to balance? If so how?

Well I remember about the group before how we moved the paper clips real close to the fulcrum but I was going to tell the group but I forgot. When we were weighing the washers it balanced.

Andy says that he remembered a technique that might have helped his group to get the scale to balance, but he never told them.

Interestingly, Andy's group also received procedural assistance from the group that went before them in another activity and Mark writes about it in this journal entry:

Today we had to make a scale with straws and two pieces of wood and measure paper clips. For a while we couldn't get the straws to balance. Then John came over and said you have to put a paper clip on each side and it worked. Then I tried to measure the paper clips. The straws broke. Then Andy, Matt, and Carole and me tried to put it back together and then science ended. I learned that you have to play your role.

What did you learn about the center of gravity?

It has to [not finished] I learned that it is the middle [this whole sentence crossed out] It's the middle of something.

Because this type of help was so beneficial, Caryn began to ask if the reporter had any advice for next group. One of the task cards presented quite a problem to Mia's group, who had devoted valuable time to deciphering what they were supposed to do. At the end of her report, Caryn asked if she had anything else to say:

MIA: Yes. I wanted to say that when you go to that group, you should . . . we did not have enough time because we had to ask Ms. McCrohon a lot of things because we . . . we just didn't know some things, and we had to ask Ms. McCrohon.

CARYN: That's OK. They had a hard time reading the card.

MIA: So when you go there, you . . . you should try reading it before you go to Ms. McCrohon. That's all I wanted to say.

Conceptual Links Across a Unit

Not only do children learn procedures from one another as units progress, they also build richer concepts as they experience and talk about the various tasks. Several examples come from the unit on balance and structure in which there are multiple activities that concentrate on balance and several more in which children construct structures from straws.

The first example occurred during a wrap-up about a balance activity. Most children at this age operate with a weight theory. Simply put, if you put something heavy on one side of a balance scale, the side that it is on will go down. However, many activities are designed to help them discover that distance from the fulcrum is also a factor they must consider. In the transcript that follows, Dina, the reporter, is talking about a task in which they use a balance fashioned from a rectangular piece of pegboard suspended from a board by a nail. Children hang various objects from different holes in the pegboard, observing what happens. Other groups have worked with a pegboard on a block which functions like a seesaw, straws that balance on wooden blocks, and a life-sized seesaw on which they themselves balance.

DINA: Well we used washers and when we put some on the other side and then the same amount on the other side it just tipped over.

CARYN: If you put the same amount on each side it tipped over?

DINA: Yeah.

CARYN: Were they on the same hole?

DINA: No.

CARYN: No. When it tipped over was the heavy thing hanging closer or further away from the fulcrum?

DINA: Further.

CARYN: Further away. Well that would make sense to me because that's the way it always has been. All the groups that I look at . . . the further thing . . . the furthest it is away from the fulcrum it has gone down. Do you know why?

Here Caryn is deliberately making the connection between this activity and others that the children have done. She says that it happens in "all the groups." Caryn then goes on to ask "why?" and another child from the group ventures this explanation:

JULIE: Oh I know why. At the end it's not in the middle so it's more.

CARYN: But why does that pull down more?

MATT: I know. I know. I know.

JULIE: Because um . . . like if I had one of these things and I just like

> put . . . put something on top of the . . . and put something on the edge it would just have more weight on that side.

CARYN: Dina said that it was equal. Equal weight.

JULIE: Yeah it was.

CARYN: But you just said there was more weight.

As the conversation unfolds, Caryn is really pushing Julie for an explanation. She knows that the children have encountered this phenomenon repeated times in different tasks and that they have many experiences that contradict their weight-only theory.

JULIE: It was equal weight because um how much things were on but the . . . how you um . . . how you put 'em on the poles.

CARYN: Right and that's what I want to know. Why does that make a difference? I want proof.

JULIE: See cuz if you put it over here it'll weigh more. *(Points to the outer end.)*

CARYN: Why? That's what I want to know. Why?

JULIE: *(Pause)* It's down at the end.

CARYN: That doesn't answer my question though.

Even at this point, Julie is using terminology which would suggest that she only is considering weight when she says "if you put it over here it'll weigh more" even though she has just claimed that they weigh the same. Again, Caryn pushes for an explanation because she truly feels that the children are on the verge of a new and more complex theory. She asks for opinions from other children.

CARYN: Do you have something to add Matt?

MATT: No.

CARYN: Dina did you? But didn't you have your hand raised? You said "I know why?"

DINA: I know why. Because it's farther away from the . . . I forget what that's called . . . yeah fulcrum and if it's farther away . . . it um . . . I mean if it's closer it kinda balances because it's um nearer the middle.

Here, Dina is able to state that the weight only seems unequal because of the distance from the fulcrum.

CARYN: Um-hm. What's the middle? What did we say yesterday, that the middle was the center of what?

DINA: Center of—*(Long pause).*

CARYN: Center point?

MARK: Of gravity.

CARYN: Of gravity.

ANDY: Um I know why um it went down because there's gravity. There's more um force. There's more force on that . . . on the ends than in the middle.

CARYN: Yeah that makes sense.

Thus far in the conversation, Caryn seems to have elicited several new components of a theory, namely that distance, as well as weight, has an impact on how things balance, and also that the force of gravity plays a role. In this particular dialogue, Caryn has been more persistent about having children come to these conclusions than she would be at the beginning of a unit, or about concepts which they less frequently encountered in the activities. Here, she feels that the group as a whole has had enough hands-on experience that they are ready to talk themselves into a new understanding. Caryn hopes they can build on their own discoveries with her guidance. The next few turns seem to demonstrate this is so. Matt raises his hand and connects this activity to the one that he did the day before in which they balanced assorted objects on the pegboard seesaw, including a small hand mirror and a large bottle of skin lotion. When they began the experiment, they were convinced that there was "no chance" of getting the two things to balance because of the discrepancy in their weight. To their surprise, they found that the two objects, when positioned correctly, would indeed balance. Matt refers to that experiment here, one that many of the other children had done on previous days:

MATT: I solved the lotion thing yesterday and the mirror.

RAMONE: I did too.

CARYN: How?

MATT: Cuz um when you move the lotion toward the mirror there's more force like over on the other side and it's making it balance.

When Matt says he moved the lotion toward the mirror, he actually means that he moved it closer to the fulcrum since the mirror was on the other side. In this response we can see that Matt is integrating the information about distance and weight, bringing in the concept of force. Next, his friend Andy asks him a question:

ANDY: How come you didn't say that?

MATT: Cuz I had to figure it out myself.

Andy's question seems to imply that Matt should have spoken up sooner, ending the prolonged questioning during wrap-up, but Matt's answer tells his friend why he delayed. It also tells us more about the value of such discussions. It is through listening to Caryn's questions and his classmates' observations and theories that he is able to come to an explanation that satisfies him. He's using the insight he gained from listening to Dina's discussion today to help him understand the activity that his group did yesterday. Because he has both rich, well-integrated, hands-on experiences and guided conversation about those experiences, he is able to "figure it out" himself. In actuality he is figuring it out in a community of inquiry, supported by his teacher.

Making Connections Happen

It is important to realize that "real-world" connections do not just happen, a realization that took us a while. Teachers must give children both permission and support to bring their lives into the classroom. Caryn first does this by asking lots of pointed questions about the real world. By doing so she makes it very clear that the classroom is part of that real world, and that experiences in and out of school are important for understanding their activities. In addition to asking questions and modeling connections for the children, Patty and Caryn must have a certain amount of trust that the stories that children tell are relevant and helpful to their understanding in some way.

For connections across activities, whether procedural or conceptual, establishing a classroom community in which children really listen to each other is perhaps the most important consideration. Here we refer to our earlier discussions of habits of mind, to an atmosphere of acceptance which shows children that people learn from their mistakes, and that allows one group to state honestly that they "messed up," while at the same time celebrating the success of their classmates who did not similarly "mess up." Because they freely discuss what went wrong, the next groups have a greater chance for success. When Mark congratulates the next group by saying "Good job!" he does so with a true appreciation of the difficulty of the task with which his group struggled, but also with the certainty that they were not in competition.

Finally, we would like to share Patty's story about Jose, a little boy in her class for whom the ability to connect what he was learning in school to his own life made a big difference in his ability to engage in school science activities.

Patty's Story

Jose entered my second grade reluctantly at best. He was very unhappy coming to a new school. He often presented me with "puzzling performances" as Karen Gallas (1996) calls the behaviors of some students who respond or act in ways that their teachers can't quite figure out. The reason Jose's performance gave me pause was because he was a very determined student, but only at times. He labored over his handwriting and stories, always concerned about his spelling and wanting to do his work, as he saw it, correctly.

Jose had not had any experience with science before coming to Goddard, so it was an area where he could have a fresh start. Often, I would see him bent over his science materials, manipulating and figuring out what needed to be done next. However, during a measurement unit, he was having a great deal of trouble both speaking and writing about what must have been abstract concepts. The whole class had a science talk about why we need measurement, and the many ways to measure. Although across the days the talk encompassed a wide variety of ideas about what and how we measure, including clocks and scales, on that first day children focused pretty much on linear measurement. Jose did not volunteer to talk. At the end of the first day of activities, when others

6–2 Jose's illustration "Helping Dad at the Store"

began to write in their journals, Jose began to look increasingly more unhappy. Then a Clark student who was working in my room sat down next to him and he began talking about his father's store. Jose drew a very detailed illustration that incorporated many different forms of measurement including a price gun, a scale, and a cash register. This illustration showed that once Jose related the topic to his life, he was able to think both widely and creatively about the topic.

7 Assessment

> **Group three and group four were very successful in doing what they needed to get done. Now it isn't that they got everything right . . . but they completed their task.**
>
> —Patty

For a very long time, being successful in school science has meant getting "everything right": words on a vocabulary quiz; facts on a chapter test; results in a planned experiment. In this framework, evaluating students was clear cut: Mark the answers correct or incorrect and compute a grade. We quote Patty's working definition of "success" from the very beginning of the year, however, because it shows that assessment in science has changed dramatically. For her second graders in the fall, working together to complete the task was their benchmark. As the year progressed, this definition of success in science evolved but it was never cut-and-dried.

It is somewhat reassuring, but not very helpful, for classroom teachers to know that assessment in science is in a state of flux. This is because the teaching of science has changed markedly, but assessment has not caught up with these changes. Open-ended tasks just do not lend themselves to paper and pencil tests; alternative assessments are currently being developed, but few are now available.

Maureen's Story About Krissy

I was in Caryn's class one afternoon while the children were working on a science unit about crystals and powders, which focuses on chemical change. Patty had already mentioned that it was hard for her students to generate questions at the beginning of this unit because they didn't know what to ask. We all knew that this was a hard one for them, both conceptually and practically. It was conceptually difficult because they didn't have much background in the topic. It was difficult on a practical or procedural level because it involved a great deal of measuring and pouring of both dry and liquid ingredients. Clipboard in hand, I sat next to Krissy, who was in a group that was making sugar crystals (rock candy). Two of her group members were busy tying a string around a pencil so that it could hang from the top of a coffee can. Another was measuring sugar. Krissy's task was to pour and measure one half cup of water.

Krissy placed a plastic drinking cup on the table in front of her and went to find a ruler. With great concentration and precision she measured the cup from bottom to top. She announced the measurement to her group, but they were all occupied in their own aspects of the task. Next, she again positioned the ruler against the cup after checking to see that the zero was at the bottom. She located the halfway mark with her finger, again being very careful and precise. Not satisfied, she set the ruler down, picked up a crayon and remeasured the cup, this time putting a mark halfway up. She then took the water jug and very carefully poured it up to the crayon mark.

Her task was to add a half cup of water. The calibrated measuring cup was never taken out of the bag of materials. Needless to say, Krissy did not add the correct amount of water to the sugar. The plastic cup probably held six ounces total, and it was much narrower at the bottom than at the top. Sugar crystals never grew on the string hung from the pencil. Rather, the sugar solution solidified into a clear mass that looked like smooth ice near the bottom of the can.

This is an interesting story from an assessment perspective because it highlights many of the issues we will discuss in this chapter. First, we are not going to consider what Krissy did not do. Of course, she was *wrong* and the experiment was a failure from the perspective of product alone, but in terms of assessing Krissy's science experience that day, we would judge her to be a success. She read the directions and had a problem to solve. Taking her task very seriously, she began to work immediately, showing that she was good at manipulating by using the tools at hand in appropriate ways. She built on skills that she had learned in a previous unit about measurement where, with guidance, she discovered things like how to orient the ruler and how to record a measurement.

Caryn used this observation as the basis for teaching the whole class how to measure liquids and introduced them to different kinds of tools, like measuring cups and spoons. She gave specific feedback to the materials manager because he never took out the measuring cup; she reminded the group about the norm that "no one of us is as smart as all of us together" because they had divided the labor in such a way that Krissy was essentially working alone. The children were not discussing the task as a group—if someone else had the ability to measure liquids they gave her no advice.

Assessing What We Value

As Maureen's story about Krissy demonstrates, the process of trying to assess students forces us to think about what's important in primary science. It only makes sense to assess what we value and what we hope that the children will come to value. Our curriculum involves cooperation, collaborative problem solving, reasoning based on hands-on experience, and learning how to talk and write science. The goal is not to have children memorize facts about science topics, but rather, to acquire the habits of mind that will enable them to be lifelong science learners.

In many ways the situation parallels that of literacy assessment. Just as traditional reading tests measure discrete skills rather than the complex interconnected cueing systems that happen in real reading, so too do science tests usually measure children's mastery of facts. Often teachers lament the fact that children can score 100 percent on a spelling test and use invented spelling for the same words in their own writing. Similarly, it's a finding of long standing that children, and even college students, will *know* about a topic on a science test but give a different explanation based on their own theory when asked in another context.

Although we do not stress facts, we do assess children's understanding of central concepts. This does not mean that we devalue facts, but rather that, for children of this age, they are less important than acquiring ways of investigating, discussing, and writing, which will become generative processes for learning about science.

We want children to become thoughtful science learners, meaning they acquire the knowledge, skills, and attitudes described in Chapter 2. Thus, we seek evidence of shared values by looking at whether children are learning how to be contributing members of a cooperative classroom environment. We look for instances when they do or do not observe the norms or play their role in the group. We note whether they can discuss their ideas openly and build on the thinking of others. We also observe whether they demonstrate certain attitudes such as a willingness to pose questions or openness to other points of view. In addition, our conception of thoughtfulness also includes skills such as observing and measuring, and knowledge of scientific concepts, especially the "big ideas" of the units that Caryn and Patty teach.

Since the wrap-up discussion is such an important component of the cooperative classroom as a way to share ideas on both the practical and conceptual levels, we also carefully review each child's performance as reporter to see signs of growth in their willingness to report and in the strategies they use. Are they able to give a procedural recount? Do they tell what happened and then go on to reasoning talk with Patty and Caryn? Although preparing reports is supposed to be a collaborative effort, after the initial turn reporters usually voice their own thinking, so we can assess them as individuals.

Listening to What the Children Say (and Write)

As you can tell from Krissy's story, a great deal of our assessment data is based on observation of the children while they are working in groups. Caryn and Patty are able to spend time observing groups and taking notes because they "delegate authority" to children through the roles and norms. When roles are being played and norms are being observed, the classroom generally runs smoothly enough for the teachers to step back and watch carefully, compiling anecdotal records about what they see. On the occasions when Leslie and Maureen have been in their classrooms, the teachers have had the luxury of two extra pairs of eyes. For example, Maureen related her observation of Krissy to Caryn, who used the information for assessment and instruction.

The other major component of our assessment data comes from listening to the children as they talk during wrap-up or write in their journals. One of the things that we most want to understand is how children grow in their ability to answer the question "how do you know?" According to *Benchmarks for Science Literacy* (1993), "The question 'How do you know?' should become routine—children should come to expect it to be asked and should feel free to ask it of others. . . . By the end of the second grade students should know that people are more likely to believe your ideas if you can give good reasons for them" (232).

Patty and Caryn listen carefully to how students justify their statements or provide evidence to buttress their claims and theories in reasoning episodes. In Chapter 4 we explained the three categories into which children's justifications fall. We will use the categories of observation, tool, and theory to organize the assessment examples that follow.

It should be noted that Caryn and Patty also look for the use of these three categories while watching children in their groups. Both observation and tool are strategies that children frequently use independently as they interact and converse with their peers. We have found spontaneous theory talk to be much less frequent, but it is noted when observed in groups. When children are working in groups, however, their actions suggest their theories and careful observation can enable Patty and Caryn to infer what the children are thinking to later be discussed in wrap-up. For instance, if they are working with a balance scale and they insist that one of the weights should be moved closer to the fulcrum, an observer could assume that they are basing that action on a theory that includes distance as well as weight.

Assessing Reasoning Based on Observation

According to *Benchmarks for Science Literacy* (1993), "By the end of second grade, students should know that: Objects can be described in terms of the materials that they are made of (clay, cloth, paper, etc.) and their physical properties (color, size, shape, weight, texture, flexibility)" (76). We feel that children not only acquire the ability to describe accurately, but they also learn to use their observations to give justifications for what they say. Caryn and Patty often hear children using this skill when they report.

The following example comes from a unit about shapes, in which Caryn wants the children to know what a polyhedron is. As an orientation, she had told them they could consider a piece of paper a flat shape and a ball a polyhedron. Later, as they categorized other shapes, they examined each one to see if it was more like the paper or the ball. In this excerpt, Caryn is asking the reporter to categorize a rectangular plastic weight that hangs on a balance scale. Although it is three dimensional, it is rather thin. Her question turns out to be difficult for Ramone:

CARYN: What would you think this is? This is one of the weights from our balance beam. Would you say this is a flat shape or a polyhedron?

RAMONE: *(Long pause)* Hm. Well *(Long pause)* I think this is in between.

Given the shape that he was assessing Ramone's answer is a reasonable one, but of course it doesn't give Caryn the information she needs to assess his understanding of categories of shapes. However, before he responds, there is a long pause during which he carefully inspects the object, looking especially at its width. Caryn notices this, and then talks about it:

CARYN: I think it's very interesting what I just saw you do, Ramone.

RAMONE: What?

CARYN: Ramone took a look at this weight, this ten-gram weight that goes on our balance scale, and he also looked at this piece of paper. And he looked at it from this side, and he looked at this from the side. Right? Is that what you did?

RAMONE: Um-hm.

CARYN: Is there a difference?

RAMONE: Yes.

CARYN: What's the difference?

RAMONE: This one's [the paper] skinnier than this [the weight].

Here Caryn explicitly points out that Ramone is carefully observing to make a comparison, using a piece of paper as a benchmark just like the whole class did before. By making this known to the entire class, she is using specific feedback to call attention to two important strategies in science: One is close observation; the other is that observations are not made in isolation, but are based on theory. That is, he judged the weight in relation to a prior definition of the paper as flat. He has a focused reason for his observational comparison. Ramone's use of these skills becomes part of Caryn's assessment of his performance.

Assessing Reasoning Based on Tools

The second category of justification is tool, which is defined by children's demonstrating with concrete objects, or by their use of "psychological tools" such as counting and measuring. Patty and Caryn consider it an important science ability for the children to be able to give reasons for their responses which include concrete examples. In addition, *Benchmarks for Science Literacy* (1993) states that, "By the end of second grade students should know that numbers and shapes can be used to tell about things." We consider this kind of justification to be within the tool category.

As the reporter of the group that converted millimeters to centimeters, Luke has given his report as though they had worked on a series of separate problems. His answers are all correct, but Caryn wants to know if he understands the principle of conversion, either multiplying or dividing by ten:

CARYN: Well, did you find any kind of patterns or something that helped you get those answers?

LUKE: Well, the first time, I think it was um ah millimeters, I can't remember.

CARYN: Well, can you tell me what's bigger, a centimeter or a millimeter?

LUKE: I think a *(Long pause)* millimeter? I can't remember what one.

CARYN: I think that maybe when this group moves on, they might be able to find that answer out. I don't know if you you I want to tell you the answer or if you want to try to discover it on your own.

LUKE: Um *(Long pause)* Tell me the answer.

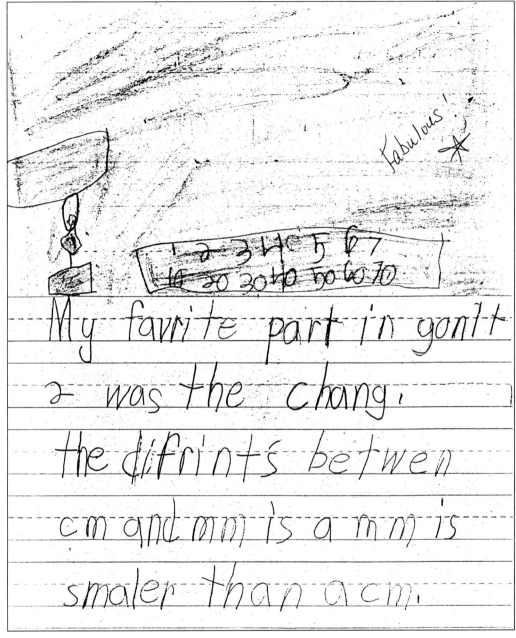

My favrite part in gonlt 2 was the chang. the difrints betwen cm and mm is a mm is smaler than a cm.

Fabulous!

7–1 Colleen's journal about measurement

CARYN: You really want to know?

ANDY: I know the answer. I know.

LUKE: Yes.

ANDY: I know.

LUKE: Andy?

ANDY: We learned that there's 10 millimeters in a centimeter, so a centimeter must be bigger.

When Luke does not immediately answer her first question, Caryn tries to ascertain if he knows the more basic fact about which unit of measurement is bigger. He answers incorrectly, but he is not sure, and Caryn simply reminds him that he will have more opportunities to work with the concepts as he moves into other related activities. While she thinks aloud about the pros and cons of giving Luke the information versus giving him more time to discover it on his own, Luke asks for the answer which Andy volunteers to provide. Not only does Andy tell which is bigger, but he gives the mathematical reason behind his assertion. This report has given Caryn quite a bit of assessment information. Luke clearly has some confusion, and though he has been told the answer by his classmate, will profit from the additional opportunities to learn about millimeters and centimeters for himself. Andy, on the other hand, can be considered to know this information. Equally important, though, is the fact that he gave an excellent explanation using the tool of counting to justify his response. In this case Caryn can assess not only what the two boys know, but also how well they can make their thinking public.

The next example is one in which Rodney, the reporter, is talking about the balance scale. You have read portions of his report in Chapter 4, where we discussed the collaborative questioning that takes place. As the report begins, Rodney is being very vague in his description:

RODNEY: *(Long pause)* Hm. OK in our group we um hadda balance something . . . the weights and we hadda balance two on each thing. Like say a ten gram on the same thing. Like say if um . . .

CARYN: I don't think they know what you mean by thing.

RODNEY: Like you put the gram—wherever that thing is *(Pause; Caryn gets the balance scale and puts it on the floor)* yeah that! . . . let me look at it.

CARYN: I thought that that might help. That's why I said if you needed to bring up your materials to help explain you could bring them up.

MARK: It's called a scale Rodney.

RODNEY: . . . A scale.

CARYN: Do you want to put it on the floor in front of you? Why don't you show it so the kids can see the numbers OK?

RODNEY: *(Begins to demonstrate)* I put just a weight here and then you put this thing right here and it'd be even cuz it's on the same numbers. Say I put that one there.

CARYN: Would you speak a little louder?

RODNEY: OK say I put this one right here that'd be out cuz if it's out it's going down there. Cuz the balance goes down, not in . . . down like that.

ALYCIA: Like the higher the number goes . . .

RODNEY: *(Interrupts)* Yeah! The lower it goes [meaning the balance arm].

After Rodney's confusing first turn, Caryn asks him to be more explicit. She gives him the tool with which to demonstrate what he's talking about. His language is highly dependent on the physical object, but he is able to show first that equal weights on the same numbers (meaning the same distance from the fulcrum) are balanced. He then uses the same equal weights, with one farther out, to make one side go down. His demonstration is a success, as attested to by his classmate Alycia, who begins to state a theory that "the higher the number goes. . . ." Rodney, who seems to have had an insight, marked by his excited "Yeah!", interrupts and completes the theory by stating, "The lower it goes." Both the demonstration and the well-phrased beginning offered by Alycia enable Rodney to state a theory about balance that considers distance from the fulcrum. In this case it is not only the reporter about whom Caryn gains valuable assessment information, but also the child who co-constructed the theory with him. It is obvious from what they both contribute that they are beginning to consider the effect of distance on balance.

The next example also shows how wrap-up can be a rich context for assessment. This is from the unit on shapes, about an activity in which the children were learning about circumference and diameter:

MARK: *(Long pause)* Well, in our group we didn't understand the card at first. And then Matt went up and asked the teacher, and um we only got to measure one thing.

CARYN: But the point is that no one understood, and a facilitator played his job, came up to me, and was then able to go back and explain everything.

MARK: Yup.

CARYN: So we saw what happened when a facilitator in the last group didn't play her job. Things didn't work out. But a facilitator that did play his job, they were able to end up understanding and at least measuring something. Did you come up with a definition of circumference and diameter?

MARK: Umm . . . Yeah.

ANDY: Mark you've gotta use like an example.

MARK: *(Picks up a plastic lid)* A diameter is going that way, like that. The circumference is going around like that. Around it.

This excerpt begins with talk about role playing, with Caryn giving positive specific feedback to the facilitator. Next, she asks for definitions of the two terms. Before Mark can begin, he gets some good advice from Andy, and then starts to demonstrate with a plastic lid by making a line across with his finger and then moving his finger around the edge. Caryn has two important pieces of assessment information as a result of this exchange: First, she knows that Mark understands what diameter and circumference are because he can show using the lid as a tool. She also knows that Andy understands an important skill in science: that you often explain by giving an example.

Assessing Reasoning Based on Theories

Benchmarks for Science Literacy (1993) says about second graders, "A premium should be placed on careful expression, a necessity in science, but students at this level should not be expected to come up with scientifically accurate explanations for their observations. Theory can wait" (10). We both agree and disagree with this statement.

We agree that children should not be expected to come up with theories that are scientifically accurate, any more than they should be expected to read or write in the same way that adults do. Research on children's naive theories (sometimes called misconceptions) has demonstrated that there are theories that many children of certain ages have in common (Osborne and Freyberg 1985). This research has shown that children are not empty vessels to be filled with whatever facts we choose to dole out, but rather, that they actively process new information in light of their current theories. The examples above show that children are using theories, whether implicit or articulated. We expect a developmental progression in which their theories become refined and more closely approximate those of adults, but we do not expect they will hold the conventional theory after one unit on a topic.

We do not agree that "Theory can wait," nor *will* it wait if children are encouraged to talk about their experiences and ideas. It is important for children to build theories and begin to tie their theories to justifications and explanations. When assisted by Caryn and Patty children *do* state theories about why certain things happen in their activities. In terms of assessment, Caryn and Patty are interested in the thinking that children do, seeking evidence that they are beginning to generalize beyond one experience and are looking for patterns which may explain what they have seen or done.

The following series of popcorn reports illustrates how a teacher might listen with an eye toward assessment of children's theory building. The first popcorn report began with the reporter, Rick, telling what the group did. He reports about how the popcorn tasted and who got to try it, both things that are important to the children. Caryn acknowledges the tasting and then asks him to tell what they did:

CARYN: Rick, could you tell the class about the uh experiment you did after you popped the popcorn the first or second time?

RICK: Oh the last time we added more oil and we kept waiting and waiting and waiting and it didn't pop and then we took it out and then . . .

CARYN: Do you think it would have popped?

SAM: No.

RICK: Yeah the first time it popped.

CARYN: Anyone else in that group need to add anything? Sam?

SAM: The second time or the third or the fourth time when we added two drops of oil and . . . but when we put all the oil over it the . . .

CARYN: So what would happen if you didn't put any oil over it?

RICK: It popped. It made a noise. It jumped up a little.

Caryn's question helps Rick to establish a result, namely that they added more oil and had to wait because the popcorn was not popping. Although Rick has talked about the amount of oil as a variable, he has not expressed a theory about *why* the amount of oil changed the outcome. He simply relates the observation that when they added more oil, they "kept waiting . . . and it didn't pop." When Caryn asks another question that could prompt a prediction (that arises from a theory) Rick offers another observation. Caryn then elicits input from Sam, a member of Rick's group:

CARYN: Sam you want to say something. I know I want to hear it. You told me in the group. What does the foil do when you put the foil over the top of the popcorn?

SAM: Keeps the heat in.

CARYN: Keeps the heat in. Do you think that it makes . . . what does that make the popcorn do?

SAM: Pop.

CARYN: Pop what? Do you think it would pop faster or pop slower?

SAM: Faster.

CARYN: Faster . . . and why?

SAM: *(Looks at the ceiling)* Well if . . . if you didn't have um foil over it the heat would be coming out.

CARYN: Uh-huh!

In response to Caryn's question, Sam offers a theory about why the foil made a difference, that it "keeps the heat in." The fact that he uses a present-tense verb marks it as a theory; he is not talking just about what has already taken place in his activity. Caryn then asks him a series of questions that helps him establish the connection between the heat and the popping corn. Here, his theory is marked by the impersonal "you" and the modal verb "would." Also, his sentence construction takes an if/then form, with "then" understood: "If you didn't have foil over it [then] the heat would be coming out."

In the next day's popcorn report, Wally, the reporter, begins with a kid-salient detail: who ate it. Caryn then asks about the amount of oil in the test tube:

WALLY: We did popcorn. The first one popped and the last one burned. I ate the first one.

CARYN: All right well let me ask you this: What happened when you added more oil to your popcorn?

WALLY: It took longer.

CARYN: It took longer. Could you tell us why that you think it took longer?

WALLY: I have absolutely no idea.

CARYN: OK, J. P., you're from that group. Do you have any idea why it took longer?

J. P.: Because it took longer to heat up the oil.

CARYN: It took longer to heat up the oil. Very good.

Here, unlike Rick, Wally does not merely relate the observation that it took a long time when they added more oil. He makes a specific comparison with the first time when they added only one drop, marked by the word "longer." Once this result is established, Caryn asks him why. His response is an excellent example of the honesty discussed before. He is perfectly comfortable saying that he has no idea. Since Wally does not offer any reason, she asks J. P., a group member, who gives the explanation "it took longer to heat up the oil." Caryn repeats and positively evaluates this response. You have probably noticed that this report is very close to the Initiation-Response-Evaluation (IRE) pattern of traditional classroom discourse. Caryn asks a question to which she knows the answer (Initiation), gets a response, and then positively evaluates the answer because it matches what she was hoping he would say.

As the units progress and Caryn and Patty try to elicit children's theories, they ask much more focused questions. This happens when Caryn and Patty think the children have had sufficient experience with the activities and when they can reasonably assume the children might know something, like heat as the source of change in these examples. As the teachers narrow the discourse space they use questions to which they know the answers in an attempt to find out if the children know. These qualities of assessment talk are very different from wrap-up talk in which Caryn and Patty ask broad and genuine questions. Notice, however, that the children still do not react as though this is a testing situation, as evidenced by Wally's comfort in admitting that he doesn't know.

Later, Caryn introduces a new question, namely what this activity has to do with change, one of the themes of the unit:

CARYN: Well the name of this unit is measurement and change. Can anyone tell me what happened to the popcorn kernel? . . . How did it change? *(No response)* How did it change? . . . Hessa do you have any idea?. . . How did it change? *(Hessa shrugs)* You watched it happen. J. P.?

J. P.: Well two of 'em popped and one just burnt. Steven took that one. Two popped and one burnt. The difference is that they didn't stay the same.

CARYN: They didn't stay the same once you put them under _____

J. P.: Fire.

CARYN: You heated them up. Very good.

In answer to this question, J. P., a member of Wally's group, offers a comparison between what happened to the popcorn the three times they did it, saying that two popped and one burned. He does say that, "The difference is that they didn't stay the same," but he does not specifically relate this contrast to the process of change. Caryn helps him connect this difference to the heat, by leaving a blank for him to fill in to complete her proposition. This is a very uncharacteristic speech pattern in wrap-up, but one that is common in many classrooms. This "fill-in-the-blank" sentence is a clear indication that she is looking, if not for a single correct response, at least a very narrow array of acceptable answers. Although Caryn rephrases his sentence as "You heated them up," his response, "fire" is within the acceptable range, as evidenced by her positive evaluation, "Very good." In this report, however, he never explicitly discusses heat as the mechanism for the change.

On the last day of the activity the report does not have an auspicious beginning. The first eight turns (which we have omitted) concern an argument in the group. Then Caryn redirects the report to the science activity:

CARYN: Would you like to explain what you did?

MORRIS: Um we . . . we let the test tube go around and first . . . the first time we were doing the popcorn it burnt so we had to . . . we had to do it over again.

CARYN: Why do you think it might have burned?

MORRIS: There was too much oil in it.

CARYN: Too much oil? What about the second time? What made it right?

MORRIS: Um . . . um there was less oil in it.

CARYN: Could you tell them what happened about the tinfoil Morris?

MORRIS: Um . . . the first time we forgot to put the tinfoil on and the second time we put it on and it worked the second time probably because the tinfoil was on and no air can get in.

CARYN: Um-hm.

MORRIS: Popped faster.

CARYN: It would pop faster because . . . would it get hotter, colder, warmer?

MORRIS: Hotter.

CARYN: Hotter? Because the tinfoil is _____?

MORRIS: On.

CARYN: On it. Anything else you want to add? *(Morris shakes his head)*
 What kind of change did the popcorn go through?

MORRIS: First it was regular, then it burnt, then it popped.

CARYN: Then it popped. And what made that change?

MORRIS: Um the fire.

CARYN: The fire . . . very good. The heat, didn't it. Good observations!

Here it can be seen that Morris, the reporter, discusses all three topics that had been raised earlier. First, he mentions the amount of oil: he says the popcorn burned because there was too much. Although this conclusion is not factually correct, he is consistent in his theory, saying that the next time it worked because there was less oil. Caryn does not try to correct him. She then asks about the tinfoil, to which he attributes their success with getting the kernel to pop, saying, "The first time we forgot to put the tinfoil on and the second time we put it on and it worked the second time probably because the tinfoil was on and no air can get in." Here he spontaneously gives an explanation about *why* the tinfoil was important. Caryn then asks a multiple choice question and uses another incomplete sentence with a blank to get him to complete the idea that the popcorn would pop faster because it would be hotter with the tinfoil on. Next, when asked a more open-ended question about the change, he is able to talk about a sequence of events: "First it was regular, then it burnt, then it popped." Caryn's question, "And what made that change?" shows that she accepted his answer as identifying a change by her use of the pronoun "that." In response to this question, he supplies the causal mechanism: the fire. She positively evaluates his answer and recasts it from the observational "fire" to the more theoretical "heat."

These sequential examples provide insight into how reports can yield assessment information about children's theories. By asking focused questions about the relationship between the heat and the changes that they observed, Caryn is able to support children to offer theories, thereby gathering information about their current thinking on the topic.

Journals also provide a window into children's theories. Students often choose to write definitions, and the way that they define terms can show their current level of understanding, as in this entry written by Angel:

> Today we learned that when the apple juice was poured it tasted good and we kept on putting water in it. It tasted bad.
>
> *What is dilution? What does it mean? How do you do it?*
>
> Dilution is when you mix two or more ingredients.

Here, Angel begins with a kid-salient detail, that is, how the juice tasted. Caryn is interested in his understanding of why the juice tasted "bad," so she asks about dilution. Although Angel's definition sounds quite scientific, with the phrase "two or more," it does not indicate that he knows the meaning of the term.

The assessment of children's theories is almost always tied to the "big idea" behind a unit, just as these examples involve change. This is because the underlying theme will be encountered several times as the children move through the various activities, and they have many opportunities to learn. The "big ideas" also represent central, important concepts. For instance, change is one of the topics listed in *Benchmarks for Science Literacy* (1993): "By the end of second grade, students should know that: . . . Things can be done to some materials to change some of their properties, but not all materials respond in the same way to what is done to them" (76).

Assessment in the Service of Instruction

Although Patty and Caryn do, in the end, have to assign report card grades for science, we see assessment as being in the service of teaching and learning, rather than for the purpose of evaluation. Caryn and Patty can use what they discover about children's understanding to plan new orientations or to support group activities. The story of Krissy is a case in point: After finding out the children did not know how to measure liquids, Caryn was able to teach them this skill. Caryn's instructional decision, based on this observation, was to teach the class as a whole during orientation because she assumed many children needed the information, and the skill was called for in several activities. Sometimes teaching based on observation is more individualized. For instance, if only a single child or a few students seem to require more instruction in a particular concept or strategy, Patty and Caryn might give tips as they are working in their groups. Because of the rotation of activities and the practice passing on advice to other groups, ideas given to one group are effectively put into what Lucy Calkins calls "the class pot" (1986, 189). This means that the ideas are in the room and available for children to use as they need them.

We take our ideas about assessment in the service of instruction from a base in whole language. First, Caryn and Patty try to assess from strength, to see what children can do that they can help them to build on. Instructional decisions can be made for the whole group, as Caryn's was about liquid measurement, but often they are for particular children. Here we are working within a Vygotskian framework using the concept of the Zone of Proximal Development, trying to keep just ahead of what the child can do on his or her own. Within this framework we are conscious of how both teacher talk and peer interaction can act as scaffolding for children's thinking. As the Morris examples show, he was supported by all of the previous reports and by Caryn's questions, yet he was able to spontaneously incorporate information from prior days in his report. Therefore, we always consider the total context of an activity and also the level of support the child receives. Sometimes Patty and Caryn do much of the work in a discussion, with the child contributing less; at other times, one teacher question will elicit a long, independent explanation. Very careful listening can help us to appreciate the child's current level of understanding.

Assessment of Knowledge

Although we are not interested in having children get "everything right," we are very interested that children acquire a basic foundation of scientific knowledge. We believe that the theory examples used above demonstrate this fact. We have also found journals to be a good way to find out what the children know, partly because their answers are individual and the teachers can probe for explicit understandings. Many journal entries make clear what the children do and don't understand.

Some excerpts from journals will serve to illustrate how they can also be used for assessment of children's knowledge. Here is Alycia's first entry about measurement:

In my group we made a centimeter ruler. It was fun.

How many centimeters in a meter? Think about it if you don't know.

There is 10 centimeters in a meter.

Tell me how you know that.

Andy told us.

Even though Alycia has the wrong answer, Caryn hopes she will explain her reasoning. Instead, she gives an honest answer, that she heard it from a member of her group. On that day time ran out and Caryn did not have the opportunity to respond further.

In her next entry, Alycia writes about the next measurement activity that involved using both centimeters and millimeters to get a precise measurement. Many of the children found this confusing, as Alycia clearly does:

> Today in my group I did not understand a word that Andy said. I tried to understand what he said but I couldn't.
>
> *This was hard for Andy to explain. Can you tell me something about millimeters or centimeters?*
>
> There are 10 centimeters in a millimeter.
>
> *You've got it backward. There are ten millimeters in a centimeter.*

In this entry it is clear that she knows that there is a relationship between millimeters and centimeters, but she still has it wrong. This time Caryn gives her the information.

Other children could display correct knowledge about the topic, such as Angel, who wrote:

> We learned that a centimeter is more bigger than a millimeter. There's ten mm in a cm.
>
> *How did you find that out?*
>
> Because a ten is a millimeter then a cm.
>
> *What do you mean?*
>
> We made discussion in our group. We said that a cm is bigger than a mm.

Caryn finds Angel's first response to her question understandable from a child's point of view, and from her observation of groups in action. What he means is that when you count to ten on the ruler, the last one (the ten) is a millimeter, but all ten together equal a centimeter.

Although Caryn has become an expert at interpreting what the children say and write, as the above example shows some entries present a challenge in terms of assessment, like the following written by Dennis:

> I learned about taste. It is fun! I like that taste. I had a good time. If you put water with the apple juice it is plain.
>
> *What is dilution?*
>
> WATER! You melt down the sweetness.

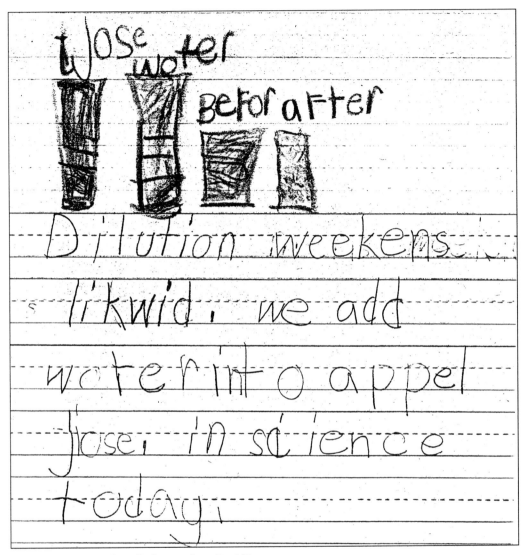

7–2 Colleen's journal: "Dilution weakens liquid"

It is clear that Dennis associates water with dilution, but it is far from clear that he knows that water weakens a liquid to which you add it. He is correct that the water that they added to apple juice made it less sweet, what he calls "plain," but it is not obvious that he has a generalized definition of dilution.

Self-assessment

Another important aspect of assessment in our program is children's self-assessment. We believe that independence in learning will result when children know when they have done a good job or when they do and don't understand. True engagement in learning, in science and other disciplines, will only come about if students can revisit questions and revise their theories, based on personal satisfaction with the fit between their predictions and results. With this we are helping students acquire metacognitive strategies that can be applied to other areas of investigation.

We also want them to acquire realistic ideas about their own abilities and those of others, to know where to turn for assistance, and what kinds of help they can offer. As we talk about multiple abilities, children begin to get a sense of who is good at what, including themselves. Recall Ross' self-appraisal, "I learned that I can be a measurer."

In keeping with the idea of "delegating authority," we often elicit from children their assessment of how well they have done on a particular day or in a specific unit. It does not take long for the children to assume this stance spontaneously, as when Ross got up to report and claimed "Today was very better than yesterday." The exchange continued:

CARYN: Very better?

ROSS: Very very better.

CARYN: Why?

ROSS: Cuz yesterday we didn't get only none of our book . . . I mean none of our reports done and today we all got our report done.

Another example comes from Alycia's journal:

Today I think we did badder than we did in the first group. In the group we were at group 2. We were badder than yesterday. I learned that asymmetrical is something that is not the same. Symmetrical is something that is the same.

Why do people need to know whether or not something is symmetrical?

So they can measure it.

Some Guidelines for Assessment

Given how complicated the issue of assessment is, it is important to remember that these guidelines are, at best, part of a work in progress.

We can emphasize some of the main points that we consider in assessment by highlighting several questions that we need to answer.

What is the child's current level of understanding and what information is she using to build her current theory? This question allows us to appreciate children's naive theories as part of a developmental continuum, rather than simply judging them to be incorrect. By examining the evidence they use to come up with their theories, we can also appreciate how they use experiences to develop their understandings, and we can assess their readiness to entertain additional information.

How much support do children need for their various tasks, either within the group during activities or during discussions? This question allows us to understand individual children's achievements better, even while they are working in collaboration with others. It also presupposes that assessment takes place when children are engaged in authentic tasks, not in artificial situations staged for assessment purposes alone. The question further enables us to assess children across a variety of contexts so that we can appreciate their range of strengths and challenges. Like Elizabeth Cohen, who designed Complex Instruction, we caution that it is not fair to assess individuals merely on the basis of their participation in groupwork because we strongly believe in the effects of status. If a child is kept on the periphery of the group because of low status, it may appear that he or she is unmotivated, uncooperative, or unable to contribute. In fact, that child may be denied access by the others. Close observation of the groups will yield this information.

How successfully did the child report for his or her group? What does the child's journal tell us about his or her current understanding of concepts? These two questions help us to see if children can begin to coordinate theory and evidence. Can they buttress an argument by using numbers and counting, estimating, measuring, manipulating, and observing? Do they show computational skills and communication skills such as explaining and demonstrating? Here we are always trying to uncover a child's sense making rather than the surface features of vocabulary or facile explanation. Occasionally, a child will use all the right words, but have little sense of what he or she means.

What abilities do children use? In keeping with the value placed on multiple abilities, we are careful not to narrow the scope of assessment to just what is written or spoken. Children who are good at manipulating, pouring, measuring, or drawing diagrams, to name just a few of the abilities, should know that these skills are important. We hope to mitigate the effects of status by showing the children that we value these abilities. If we don't include these abilities in our assessment children can reasonably conclude they don't really "count" in any meaningful way, and all our talk about honoring multiple abilities will be in vain.

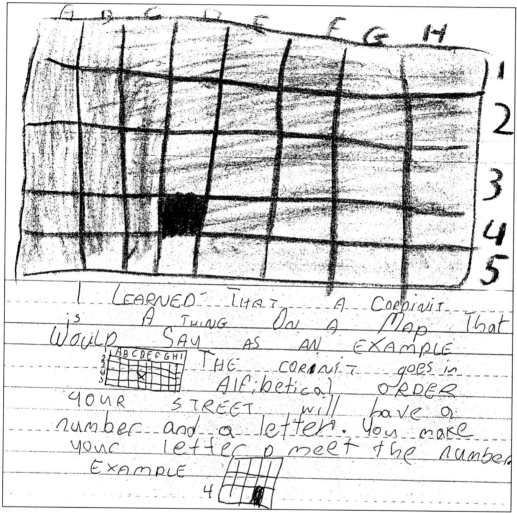

7–3 *Andy's journal explanation of how to use coordinates*

How well did children play their roles? How well did they observe the norms? We value these two questions not just as indications of social abilities, but also because they provide insight into shared values and attitudes. Do the children display curiosity, openness to ideas, and skepticism? Do they seem to have the idea that everyone is able to contribute and do science? We want to make it clear that although we greatly value groupwork, we do not give grades to the group as a whole. Elizabeth Cohen is against giving group grades for the following reason: "It has the drawback of making the peer evaluation process rather harsh. If one group member is felt to be incompetent at the task, the group is likely to forbid him or her to have any part in the product" (1994, 82). In other words, group grading can exacerbate the problems of dominance and exclusion that are crested by status.

We were gratified last year to discover that the children whom Caryn and Patty taught in their 92–93 second-grade class were very successful in the science subtest of the first Massachusetts Assessment of Educational Progress Test, which was administered in the spring of their fourth-grade year. Obviously, these children had many other intervening experiences, including two additional years of the same hands-on science program. Although Patty and Caryn share the credit for this success with all their colleagues at the Goddard School, it is still true that these children spent one formative school year doing hands-on activities and talking about them with their second-grade classmates and teachers.

We know that such tests are important for students' future success in school and we celebrate when the children do well, yet Caryn and Patty still struggle with assessment on a daily basis. The question of how to assess children's achievement in this program has been—and continues to be—a difficult but fertile one for us to contemplate. The insights we have gained apply across the curriculum. We have been forced continually to ask ourselves about what really matters. Of course we want students to learn scientific concepts and facts, but we also want them to acquire habits of mind and to gain a sense of accomplishment, so they come to realize science is something *they can do.*

8 Stories of Ross

Quite ordinary people can be good at science. To say this is not to deprecate science but to appreciate ordinary people. But to be good at science one must want to be.

Peter Medawar, The Limits of Science

According to linguist Jay Lemke, who has studied high school science classes, "If some students do badly in science it is not because science is so difficult or they are so dumb. It is because the way in which science is presented to them seems too unfamiliar or too unlike what they have been taught for them to find it interesting or valuable" (1990, 139). We have searched for ways to help children become science learners who build theories, ask questions, and make meaningful connections, so that they will not, as Lemke puts it "do badly in science."

We quote Peter Medawar because we believe all children can learn to "be good at science" if we help them develop a personal investment, so that they will *want* to be good at science. We stress the development of a community of second-grade scientists in which children can acquire not only conceptual knowledge and procedural skills, but also scientific habits of mind. The shared values of this community gradually become individual children's attitudes about learning, and about themselves as learners.

The most important mechanism for establishing this community is dialogue, in both talk and writing, for two reasons: First, following Vygotsky, we believe in the importance of speech for children's development. Second, we also believe, as Lemke claims, "the mastery of a specialized subject like science is in large part mastery of its specialized ways of using language" (21). The children we work with say things like, "It tasted too yuk cuz it was mushy." Certainly the child who offered this description is far from the "mastery" of the language of science to which

163

Lemke refers, yet children's introduction to science is also an introduction to how to *talk science* and *write science*.

The following two stories about Ross, who was taught by both Patty and Caryn, offer a way to speculate about the outcomes of our approach to talking and writing within the context of hands-on science teaching.

Caryn's Story: Ross in Second Grade

On the first day of school in 1994, Ross' grandmother and father brought him into school an hour late. He refused to come inside the classroom. He stood outside, leaning against the lockers, trying hard not to cry in front of his new teacher. He even punched a locker, emphasizing his point that he was absolutely not going into the classroom. He wouldn't speak above a whisper to me, so after about five minutes of trying to coax Ross into joining the class, I went back into the classroom and asked if anyone in the class knew Ross. Many students started shouting "Yeah, Ross is here!" I told the class that he was having a hard time coming into the room and asked if anyone wanted to go out into the hallway and talk to him. Several children volunteered. Since I had only known my class for an hour, I randomly chose two boys, Mark and Luke, to go out in the hall and talk to Ross. They very quickly coaxed Ross into the room, where he smiled until it was time to go home. I do not know what the boys said to him, but he came into the room willingly and enjoyed his first day of second grade. At the end of the school day, I wrote a note home to his grandmother and his father, who were worried about him when they left. I told them not to be concerned because Ross was happy for the rest of the day. After that first day of school, I never worried about Ross' reluctance to be a part of our classroom community. However, I did have other concerns about Ross and how he viewed himself.

Ross turned out to play a large role not only in our classroom community but also in helping me think through my teaching philosophy. He confirmed my belief that cooperative learning is essential to successful math and science programs in urban elementary schools. Ross was a small, quiet, and somewhat timid child, unless he was playing with friends at recess. He had very low self-esteem because of his reading difficulty. He indicated to me that he could not read and would never be able to. I asked him why, and he responded by saying, "I stayed back in first grade because I couldn't read, and I still can't read, so I can never read." Perhaps these feelings contributed to his unwillingness to come into his new second-grade classroom that first day.

Ross had difficulty with reading, yet he was extremely capable in math, very diligent in his work in science, and an accomplished writer/ illustrator. His math skills were useful in many areas, especially science, yet he did not believe that he was "good" in either math or science. He enjoyed writing, even though he had difficulty with reading. He often asked when we were going to do "Writer's Workshop" or if he could write in his journal during free time. The other students looked forward to hearing him share his latest creations. He was well-liked by all the students in the class and they were very supportive of him. They frequently reminded him of his many abilities, especially his standing in the class as the resident manipulator and measurer.

Patty's Story: Ross in Fourth Grade

I just began to teach fourth grade this year, and Ross is now in my class with many of the same children he was with in Caryn's room two years ago. Recently, he accomplished something quite remarkable. But before I tell you about that, I'd like to give you a general picture of Ross as a fourth grader. Each morning as we begin the day, children make individual choices to read or write. Ross usually chooses to read, and his reading choices span both fiction and nonfiction and include topics like insects and sports. During science, it is clear that Ross enjoys thinking and working together with others. He is observant, accurate, and deliberate in his work and in sharing his perspective with his group. He is still modest about his own abilities, though, as his cheeks flush red when it is acknowledged he is doing some "good thinking."

A few weeks ago I decided to introduce a math project called "What's in a glyph?" It is a complex, multistep activity that involves introducing the students to the idea of representation in both graphic displays, such as bar charts or line graphs, as well as pictures. In order to gather information to represent, the class collected data on transportation to school, languages spoken at home, family pets, birthdays, favorite sports, and favorite subjects. The students worked in small groups to obtain this information from group members and decide how they should report their results graphically to the class. After we worked together to complete the graphs, each child had to make a personal *glyph* to represent all of their personal data. They accomplished this by constructing paper hot air balloons with each feature of the balloon corresponding to one of the categories of data. For example, the shape of the basket represented how children got to school; the pattern on the basket represented languages spoken at home; the number of strings attaching the basket to the balloon represented favorite subject, and so on. This was a hard project for the children. The class had been working for twenty minutes as I traveled from group to group to check and see if the children had any questions. When I arrived at Ross' group, he had almost completed his entire project, while the other students were still in the beginning steps. I was surprised because I knew that this was a difficult task for students, one that involved the idea of representation. I didn't expect students to finish quickly, and planned to spend more than one class period on both the graphs and the hot air balloon glyphs. I stopped the class and asked if Ross would share his glyph. He agreed and went on to carefully describe exactly what he had done. I then suggested that students ask Ross questions, and he told them what each of the symbols stood for. It was clear that Ross had developed important skills such as working independently, breaking a task into steps, and explaining clearly to others.

When I completed writing this story, I asked Ross if I could share it with the other children in our class. He agreed and as I read the story aloud to the group he sat shyly looking satisfied and pleased. When I finished, I asked if there were any comments. Raja raised her hand and reminded us of a multiplication activity that we had done the other day. She remembered that Ross understood a key aspect of that activity and shared information that enabled the class to go on to the next step. Again, it was a difficult activity that required the students to graphically display six times twenty-two. They were stumped by this question. As twenty-five children sat quietly considering how to represent this multiple pattern, Ross slowly raised his hand into the air. He quietly began explaining how you would illustrate a multiple pattern on a chart. After Ross' explanation lots of hands began to go up to discuss what he had said. Ross is known by his classmates as having many skills and abilities that fall under the heading of "good thinking." He takes pride in practicing them each day when he comes to school.

What Can the Case of Ross Teach Us?

Ross' story is a poignant one: He is a child who has been admired by classmates, teachers, and researchers alike. We do not tell his story just because it is moving, though. Ross is in some ways an exemplar of what we hope to see as children participate in science learning communities. As we mentioned in the introduction, we define learning broadly, in the same way as Barbara Rogoff does, "a transformation in participation" (1994, 209). Ross' participation has changed over time in many ways. We will discuss two here: The first involves the shift in attitude he experienced as a result of participating in a science community that values multiple abilities. Ross is a good example of a child coming to adopt the values of his community, not just values toward science but also attitudes about himself as a student of science. The second focuses on Ross' personal intellectual accomplishments in building on his early abilities as a manipulator and measurer (both more physical kinds of maneuvering) to achieve a level of mental manipulation in the form of symbolism. Although each aspect is taken separately, they are intimately related to one another.

As Caryn's stories about Ross indicate (both here and in Chapter 3), he was his own worst critic. When he was in Caryn's second grade, he frequently felt that he was not "good" at anything in spite of many reminders to the contrary from Caryn and his classmates. Ross was not a student who had difficulty cooperating with others, a common obstacle for most second graders, but rather, he seemed to need support in taking on other values associated with his science community. Specifically, Ross needed to see himself as a thoughtful contributor who had important things to share. In this regard Ross is a vivid example of what most human beings require in order to function in the world: a sense of purpose and agency. Ross, like all of us, needs to know that what he does can make a difference in the quality of his life and those around him. This is first and foremost an attitude, but as we can tell from Ross' experience, his own attitudes were clearly related to the values of his community. Since reading is typically one of a few highly prized skills in school settings and Ross had difficulty with reading in school, he quickly adopted an attitude toward himself as an unsuccessful student. It took Ross' community a long time working with him before he saw that there were other abilities that mattered to them too. Although still shy and modest about his abilities in fourth grade, he is continuing to develop a sense of himself as a competent student with support from his community. In turn, this sense of self has led to more of a willingness on his part to nominate himself to help the class as they struggle with difficult concepts, particularly in math and science.

Another shift that Ross has experienced is in the cognitive realm. Caryn's second-grade students quickly noticed that Ross was a superb manipulator and measurer. He had highly developed fine motor skills that allowed him to succeed in many tasks that required careful, deliberate, and delicate movements, such as untangling necklaces. He also had a sense of how physical tools such as rulers could be used to provide a way of ensuring that lines were spaced equidistant from one another. These abilities, which involve manipulation and tool use on a physical level, were the building blocks for what we see Ross accomplishing in fourth grade with the glyph activity, which required highly developed mental manipulation and use of symbolic tools.

There are many kinds of tools that structure human activity and interaction. We have discussed tools as one of the ways students justify their findings to Caryn and Patty. We have defined tools as culturally sanctioned strategies (such as counting) or devices (such as rulers) that help amplify students' sensory information. We discussed how language functions both as a tool for communicating meaning and as a way to regulate one's own behavior. Language, as we described, serves as a link between the social and intellectual world.

But what is language really? It is a complex set of representations such that all speakers of a particular language understand that some configuration of scribbles on a page or sounds out of a mouth stand for concrete objects (a chair) or abstract ideas (democracy). The importance of the symbolic nature of language is seen early on, with caregivers constantly naming objects in the environment and playing games that require young children to name things too. But the notion of symbolism is never discussed as such, and is an intellectually demanding idea to grasp.

This is what makes Ross' ability to understand and execute the necessary steps to complete his glyph project so remarkable: Ross had to take his understanding of language a step further than simply using language to communicate with others or regulate his own behavior. He had to consciously think about and manipulate language itself as a symbolic tool. Beyond that, he had to recognize that one could *invent* one's own symbols to correspond to both linguistic representations and their referents. Therefore, he was able to understand that math as a favorite activity can be represented not just by the written convention of *m a t h,* but also with five pieces of string that would connect his basket to his balloon. Ross also understood that if someone had three pieces of string it meant that they did not like math best but instead preferred social studies. These are complex mental operations that Ross carried out independently and in a relatively short period of time. Ross has expanded his second-grade repertoire of physical manipulation and tool use to include an understanding of symbols as mental tools for organizing the world, or at least representing a series of qualities that describe himself and his classmates.

We believe that these stories about Ross encapsulate most of what we have written about in this book. We began by discussing scientific habits of mind represented by knowledge, skills, values, and attitudes. You can see the complex interplay of all of these characteristics developing in Ross because he has worked in and continues to benefit from a supportive community of fellow science learners.

In closing, to again quote John Dewey's speech to the American Association for the Advancement of Science in 1909: "I believe that the attitude toward science should be fixed during the earlier years of life." We feel that this has happened for Ross and for the other children whom Patty and Caryn teach. Unfortunately, many students are, at least statistically, unlikely candidates for success in school science: girls, minority students, and second-language learners are groups who have been historically excluded. We are trying to change this picture through our practices. By helping these students to talk and write about their experiences, we hope to instill a generative engagement with the habits of mind, tools, and ideas of the discipline so that they will not be denied entry into the world of science as they get older. Although each child is a unique individual, to us, they all are the "ordinary people" about whom Medawar writes. We trust that they can and will be good in science because they want to be.

References

AICKEN, F. 1991. *The Nature of Science.* Portsmouth, NH: Heinemann.

AMERICAN ASSOCIATION FOR THE ADVANCEMENT OF SCIENCE. 1993. *Benchmarks for Science Literacy.* New York: Oxford University Press.

ATWELL, N. 1987. *In the Middle.* Portsmouth, NH: Boynton/Cook.

BAKHTIN, M. M. 1981. *The Dialogic Imagination.* Austin: University of Texas Press.

BARNES, D. 1992. *From Communication to Curriculum.* 2d ed. Portsmouth NH: Boynton/Cook.

BARNES, D., AND F. TODD. 1995. *Communication and Learning Revisited: Making Meaning Through Talk.* Portsmouth, NH: Heinemann.

BEVERIDGE, W. I. B. 1950. *The Art of Scientific Investigation.* New York: Vintage.

CAIRNEY, T. 1990. "Intertextuality: Infectious Echoes from the Past." *The Reading Teacher* 43: 478–84.

CALKINS, L. M. 1986. *The Art of Teaching Writing.* Portsmouth, NH: Heinemann.

CAZDEN, C. B. 1988. *Classroom Discourse: The Language of Teaching and Learning.* Portsmouth, NH: Heinemann.

CHINN, C. A., AND W. F. BREWER. 1993. "The Role of Anomalous Data in Knowledge Acquisition: A Theoretical Framework and Implications for Science Teaching." *Review of Educational Research* 63: 1–49.

COHEN, E. G. 1994. *Designing Groupwork: Strategies for the Heterogeneous Classroom.* New York: Teachers College Press.

———. 1984. "Talking and Working Together: Status, Interaction, and Learning." In *The Social Context of Instruction: Group Organization and Group Processes,* edited by P. L. Peterson, L. C. Wilkinson, and M. Hallinan, 171–87. San Diego: Academic Press.

COHEN, E. G., R. A. LOTAN, AND L. CATANZARITE. 1990. "Treating Status Problems in the Cooperative Classroom." In *Cooperative Learning:*

Theory and Research, edited by S. Sharan, 203–29. New York: Praeger.

DEREWIANKA, B. 1990. *Exploring How Texts Work.* Rozelle, NSW Australia: Primary English Teaching Association.

DEWEY, J. 1910. "Science as Subject-Matter and as Method." *Science* 31 (787): 121–27.

DRIVER, R. 1983. *The Pupil as Scientist?* Philadelphia: Open University Press.

DUSCHL, R. A. 1990. *Restructuring Science Education.* New York: Teachers College Press.

ERICKSON, F. 1986. "Qualitative Methods in Research on Teaching." In *Handbook of Research on Teaching,* edited by M. E. Wittrock. New York: Macmillan.

GALLAS, K. 1996. Keynote address, First Annual Worcester Teachers' Ethnographic Research Forum, 1 May.

———. 1995. *Talking Their Way into Science: Hearing Children's Questions and Theories, Responding with Curricula.* New York: Teachers College Press.

GARDNER, H. 1983. *Frames of Mind: The Theory of Multiple Intelligences.* New York: Basic Books.

GOLDENBERG, C. 1992/1993. "Instructional Conversations: Promoting Comprehension Through Discussion." *The Reading Teacher* 46: 316–26.

GOULD, S. J. 1981. *The Mismeasure of Man.* New York: W. W. Norton & Company.

KARMILOFF-SMITH, A., AND B. INHELDER. 1975. "If You Want to Get Ahead, Get a Theory." *Cognition* 3: 195–212.

KUHN, D. 1993. "Science as Argument: Implications for Teaching and Learning Scientific Thinking." *Science Education* 77: 319–37.

KUHN, D., E. AMSEL, AND M. O'LAUGHLIN. 1988. *The Development of Scientific Thinking Skills.* Developmental Psychology Series. New York: Academic Press.

LABOV, W. 1970. "The Study of Language in Its Social Context." In *Language and Social Context,* edited by P. P. Giglioli, 283–308. New York: Penguin.

LATOUR, B., AND S. WOOLGAR. 1986. *Laboratory Life: The Construction of Scientific Facts.* Princeton, NJ: Princeton University Press.

LEMKE, J. L. 1990. *Talking Science: Language, Learning, and Values.* Norwood, NJ: Ablex.

MEDAWAR, P. 1984. *The Limits of Science.* New York: Oxford University Press.

MEHAN, H. 1979. *Learning Lessons.* Cambridge, MA: Harvard University Press.

MERCER, N. 1991. "Putting Context into Oracy." In *Oracy Matters,* edited by M. Maclure, T. Phillips, and A. Wilkinson, 122–32. Philadelphia: Open University Press.

MILLAR, R., AND R. DRIVER. 1987. "Beyond Processes." *Studies in Science Education* 14: 33–62.

MOLL, L. C. 1990. Introduction to *Vygotsky and Education: Instructional Implications and Applications of Sociohistorical Psychology,* edited by L. C. Moll. New York: Cambridge University Press.

OCHS, E., C. TAYLOR, D. RUDOLPH, AND R. SMITH. 1992. "Storytelling as Theory-Building Activity." *Discourse Processes* 15: 37–72.

ONOSKO, J. J., AND F. M. NEWMANN. 1994. "Creating More Thoughtful Learning Environments." In *Creating Powerful Thinking in Teachers and Students,* edited by J. N. Mangieri and C. C. Block, 27–49. New York: Harcourt Brace College Publishers.

OSBORNE, R., AND P. FREYBERG. 1985. *Learning in Science: The Implications of Children's Science.* Portsmouth, NH: Heinemann.

PALEY, V. G. 1990. *The Boy Who Would Be a Helicopter: The Uses of Storytelling in the Classroom.* Cambridge, MA: Harvard University Press.

PALINCSAR, A. M., C. ANDERSON, AND Y. M. DAVID. 1993. "Pursuing Scientific Literacy in the Middle Grades Through Collaborative Problem Solving." *Elementary School Journal* 94: 643–58.

PRATT, C. 1948. *I Learn from Children.* New York: Cornerstone Library.

REDDY, M. F. 1994. Becoming Second-Grade Scientists: A Discourse Analysis of Science Discussions. Unpublished doctoral thesis, Harvard University.

RESNICK, L. B. 1989. Introduction to *Knowing, Learning, and Instruction: Essays in Honor of Robert Glaser,* edited by L. B. Resnick, 1–24. Hillsdale, NJ: Erlbaum.

ROGOFF, B. 1990. *Apprenticeship in Thinking: Cognitive Development in Social Context.* New York: Oxford University Press.

———. 1994. "Developing Understanding of the Idea of a Community of Learners." *Mind, Culture, and Activity* 1: 209–29.

ROWE, M. B. 1978. *Teaching Science as Continuous Inquiry.* 2d ed. New York: McGraw Hill.

RUTHERFORD, F. J., AND A. AHLGREN. 1990. *Science for All Americans.* New York: Oxford University Press.

SCHIFFRIN, D. 1987. *Discourse Markers. Studies in Interactional Sociolinguistics* 5. New York: Cambridge University Press.

SHORT, K. G. 1986. "Literacy as a Collaborative Experience: The Role of Intertextuality." In *Solving Problems in Literacy: Learners, Teachers, and Researchers,* edited by J. Niles and R. Lalik, 227–32. Rochester, NY: National Reading Conference.

SHORT, K. G., J. C. HARSTE, AND C. BURKE. 1996. *Creating Classrooms for Authors and Inquirers.* 2d ed. Portsmouth, NH: Heinemann.

STATON, J., R. W. SHUY, J. K. PEYTON, AND L. REED. 1988. *Dialogue*

Journal Communication: Classroom, Linguistic, Social, and Cognitive Views. Norwood, NJ: Ablex.

THARP, R. G., AND R. GALLIMORE. 1988. *Rousing Minds to Life: Teaching, Learning, and Schooling in Social Context.* New York: Cambridge University Press.

TISHMAN, S., D. PERKINS, AND E. JAY. 1995. *The Thinking Classroom: Learning and Teaching in a Culture of Thinking.* Boston: Allyn and Bacon.

VYGOTSKY, L. S. 1987. *The Collected Works of L. S. Vygotsky.* Translated by N. Minick. Vol. 1. New York: Plenum.

———. 1978. *Mind in Society: The Development of Higher Psychological Processes.* Cambridge, MA: Harvard University Press.

WELLS, G. 1992. "What Have You Learned?: Co-constructing the Meaning of Time." Unpublished manuscript. Ontario Institute for Studies in Education, Joint Center for Teacher Development.

WERTSCH, J. V. 1991. *Voices of the Mind: A Sociocultural Approach to Mediated Action.* Cambridge, MA: Harvard University Press.

———, ed. 1985. *Culture, Communication, and Cognition.* New York: Cambridge University Press.